DANISH LITERATURE

KV-196-764

DFIE

DANES OF THE PRESENT AND PAST

DANISH LITERATURE

A Short Critical Survey
by Poul Borum

BUCKS COUNTY LIBRARY

A & B   255/81T

R 839.8109
BOR

DET DANSKE SELSKAB

COPENHAGEN 1979

Cover
Johannes V. Jensen
(drawing by Sikker Hansen)

Acknowledgement
The Danish Institute expresses
its gratitude to the publishers Gyldendal and
Politiken for permission to use photos
from their archives.

Printing
Krohns Bogtrykkeri, Copenhagen

© *Copyright 1979*
DET DANSKE SELSKAB
The Danish Institute for Information about
Denmark and Cultural Cooperation with other Nations
Kultorvet 2, DK-1175 Copenhagen K.
Tel. (45-1) 13 54 48

ISBN 87-7429-030-4

Printed in Denmark

Contents

Preliminary Remarks

This book is a short survey of contemporary Danish literature, preceded by an even shorter sketch of the first thousand years of Danish literature.

It is published by The Danish Institute whose object is to spread information about Denmark, and it is written by a literary critic for people interested in literature.

In a significant lecture on 'The Aesthetics of Literary Influence' at the second congress of the International Comparative Literature Association (reprinted in his book *Literature as System*, Princeton 1971), the American critic Claudio Guillén put it very succinctly: 'It is important . . . that the study of a topic such as, say, Dutch poetry be encouraged not for charitable but for poetic reasons.'

In other words, an interest in, say, Danish dairy associations need not oblige you to know anything about Danish literature. But if you are interested in literature, you might want to include some Danish books in your lifetime reading plan – let us say twenty classics and twenty modern books. This book should help you to make your own Top Forty list.

Unfortunately, most of the books on such a list do not exist in English translations. But some of them do, and they are listed in the bibliography. One of the main purposes of this book is, of course, to inspire translators (and publishers) to good deeds to world literature. Most of the writers mentioned in this book are represented in one or both of two anthologies:

Anthology of Danish Literature. Edited by F. J. Billeskov Jansen and P. M. Mitchell. Bilingual. Southern Illi-

nois University Press, Carbondale, Ill., 1971, paperback edition in two volumes 1972.
Contemporary Danish Poetry. Twayne, N.Y., 1977.

A very comprehensive scholarly history of Danish literature
by Professor P. M. Mitchell, the dean of Scandinavian studies
in America, was published by Gyldendal in Copenhagen in
1957. Although I tend to disagree with several of Mitchell's
evaluations of literature after 1800, I heartily recommend his
informative book.

The present short book is written by a literary critic who is
also a poet. But please note that the Danish word 'litteratur-
kritiker' means an inferior person who writes book reviews
for newspapers and magazines. An academic critic is called a
'litteraturforsker' (scholar) or 'litteraturhistoriker' (historian). The main difference, of course, is that the first sort of
critic knows that his evaluations are subjective. So you have
been warned. Inevitably a book like this is based on value
judgments. It is not an encyclopedia. But I trust that compe-
tent readers of Danish will agree with me in most cases about
inclusions and omissions and about relative placings, and
that really is as far as we can get toward objectivity: that
common agreement which is called intersubjectivity.

A few years ago the British critic *Martin Seymour-Smith*
published a monumental one-man-show called *Guide to
Modern World Literature* (Wolfe, London, 1973), in which
the Danish chapter not only had several factual mistakes, but
also some rather strange evaluations. For instance, we are
told about two of the poets of the eighteen-nineties that
Sophus Claussen 'was not a better poet than Stuckenberg' –
which is comparable to saying that Yeats was not a better
poet than A. E. Housman. I wondered how Seymour-Smith
could have formed his opinion, so I tried to look up his sources. The older anthologies of Danish poetry in English had a
few very amateurish translations of both poets, and in P. M.

Mitchell's history of Danish literature there was less than a page about Claussen – in a chapter curiously titled 'The Road to Materialism' – where after a few facts it is bluntly stated that 'many of his metaphors are indistinct to the point of being incomprehensible'. Imagine a similar statement about Yeats or Dylan Thomas in a history of English literature. An obvious explanation is that Professor Mitchell's literary taste was formed in the thirties, while later generations have obtained a more relaxed relationship with so-called 'incomprehensible' metaphors. But really, Claussen 'not a better poet than Stuckenberg' – !

One last point should be made: about novels. In my evaluation of some recent novelists, mostly 'realists' of the psychological or social-documentary schools, I know that I disagree with some critics whom I respect (and with the horde of younger trendy Marxists which dominates the Danish universities). But I do think it is a great and, perhaps, insoluble problem of practical criticism to distinguish between the novel as entertainment and the novel as art. About the classics we usually agree. Time has sorted out the valuable novels for us, and most of them are rather entertaining, too. Some of them even started as 'pure entertainment' and acquired the status of classics later. Among the enormous number of novels being poured out in our day, it is easy enough to pick out the very few works of art and to leave the vast majority of commercial reading-matter to the sociologists. But in between are all those books that want to do both, to be both artefacts and entertainments, and often fail in both functions.

Connected with this practical problem is a historical problem: it is often a little hard to see why so many contemporary writers still want to write Nineteenth Century Novels now, toward the end of the twentieth century. There was a certain time in the literary history of most smaller nations when the big panoramic novels, the National Geographic Epics, were necessary – in Denmark it happened about the turn of the

9

century with Henrik Pontoppidan, in Eastern Europe between the wars, with Reymont in Poland, Sholokhov in Russia, and Andric in Yugoslavia, and in some parts of the Third World it occurred in the fifties and sixties, e. g. Patrick White in Australia and Asturias in Guatemala. And we can certainly expect that sort of novel to be coming out of Africa and Asia in the near future. Incidentally, it is significant that all the novelists mentioned have received Nobel prizes in literature – they were great *national* writers. But to write novels today as if Proust and Henry James and Joyce and Faulkner had never existed seems rather incongruous.

This book will, I hope, show that I do not advocate novelty for novelty's sake, but I would like to tell you about *contemporary* Danish literature. Let us begin at the beginning.

Carl Kähler, M. A., has been immensely helpful in correcting the manuscript, which was written in the summer of 1977 and revised and brought up to date in January 1979.

Poul Borum

The First Thousand Years

The Middle Ages

Traditionally histories of literature compensate for the lack of masterpieces in the earlier periods of a country's literary history by hundreds of pages about pre-literature, foreign literature, non-literature and simply bad literature. In Denmark, too, literary historians have appropriated – and some of them still do – lots of material which rightly belongs to archaeology, history or philology. Actually our only contribution to world literature before the seventeenth century is the ballads. – Even they are part of comparative literature, an international genre, linked with musicology and folklore, whether in its Romantic version which sees the ballads as an expression of the communal soul or in its modern Marxist version recovering them for the repressed population.

The earliest written documents, runic inscriptions from the fifth to the tenth century, first in prose, later sometimes in verse, belong to the history of writing but are certainly not literature in our sense of the word. The mythological Edda-poems as well as the later prose Sagas belong to Iceland. There is however some reason for including the Edda mythology in a Danish literary history, not because the poems express a common Nordic pre-Christian mythology, of which there are few traces in Denmark, but because they provided much source material between 1760 and 1860, when poets believed in, or at least exploited, the notion of such a common mythological heritage.

From the eleventh century on we have documents of church and state in Latin and, little by little, in Danish, too – lives of saints, chronicles and annuals, laws and diplomatic letters. Then come the edifying and entertaining books for the layman, devotional literature, popular manuals of medicine, travelbooks and stories, mostly translated from the German. And the first attempts at poetry, rimes about saints, songs to the Virgin. Most of this pre- or non-literature develops in the same way as in most other European countries, and it would be a proper task for comparative literature to research the degrees of literariness in these documents on a supranational level. The Danish contribution does not seem to be either very great or very original.

We do, however, have some important contributions to make to the as yet uncompiled anthology of medieval Latin writing. First of all there is the clerk *Saxo*'s *Gesta Danorum* (Deeds of the Danes) from 1220 – from which Shakespeare indirectly got his story about the melancholy Dane. Saxo's voluminous work is both a tendentious reportage about recent history and a collection of mythical lore, with the Old Norse mythology retold in florid Roman Silver Age prose and verse. The Renaissance and, later, the Romantic translations of Saxo's entertaining chronicle have rightly become common property in Denmark, and the medieval scribe has contributed not a little to the Danishness of Danes, to their understanding of themselves and their place in history.

Up to the end of the eighteenth century a lot of poetry in Denmark was written in Latin, and some of it seems to have international stature. Saxo's contemporary *Anders Sunesøn* wrote an epic theological poem in 9000 hexameters called *Hexaëmeron*. The best and most productive Renaissance Latin poet was *Erasmus Laetus* (1526, 1560, 1582)* who in 1573 dedicated his poem about the first Queen Margaret of Denmark to the first Queen Elizabeth of England. In the Baroque period *Henrik Harder* (1642, 1679, 1683) wrote epigrams that can compare with his model, the Englishman John

---

* Here and throughout the book the years in parenthesis indicate birth, year of first published book, and death (if he is dead) of an author.

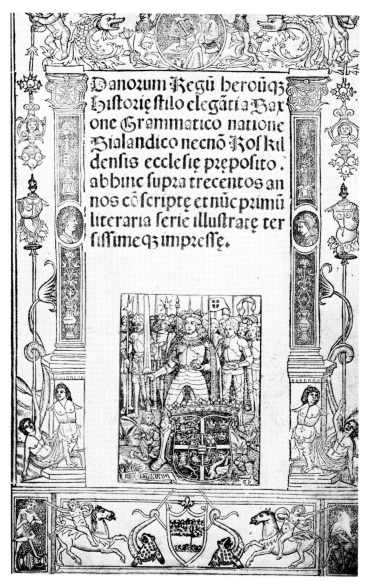

Saxo's Gesta Danorum, title page of the first printed edition, 1514.

Owen. Our greatest writer of the first part of the eighteenth century, *Ludvig Holberg*, was also an inveterate latinist who published epigrams, an autobiography and an utopian satire in the international language. (The latter two works exist in English translation).

The Ballads

The ballads, the epic dancesongs of the late Middle Ages, still a part of popular tradition in Scandinavia and Anglosaxon countries – and still being sung and danced to in the Faroes – are one of the most problematical fields of literary history. There is no doubt that at least two or three score of the Danish corpus – some 500 as opposed to the 300 of Child's collection – are poetical masterpieces. Yet just to establish a text is extremely difficult. The enormous edition of *Danmarks gamle folkeviser* (Denmark's Old Folk Ballads) which was commenced by Svend Grundtvig in 1853 and only recently completed (and is of course totally dated) gives as many versions of each ballad as possible. These may be from manuscript collections belonging to noble ladies of the Renaissance, from printed anthologies – the first of which was made in 1591 by the humanist *Anders Sørensen Vedel* (1542, 1575, 1616), who also made the first translation of Saxo's chronicle – from later broadsides, or from transcriptions of oral deliveries in the nineteenth and twentieth centuries. Which should one prefer and for what reason today when it is no longer permissable to make your own composite 'literary' version? The ballads are an anonymous genre, partly orally transmitted, and the corpus is in a horrible mess.

But if we let the philologists, historians, folklorists and musicologists have their choice, there is still a good measure of great poetry left for the literary critic. Here new problems of both aesthetics and ethics arise. The ballads were composed for performance. They are *Gesamtkunstwerke* of music, dance, interpretation and poetry, and the poetry again is a composite of epic story-telling, dramatic dialogues, and lyric colouring, especially in the refrains characteristic of Danish balladry and apparently sung by the chorus of dancers. To comprehend the ballads we must put aside our usual notions of clear demarcation between art forms, literary kinds and fictional types. We shall also have to rethink the ethical implications of these feudal lovesongs – they were made before the great 'dissociation of sensibility', which means that there is an indissoluble connection between their form and their feeling, an identity of mood and mode which we have unlearned in the last four centuries.

The literary revival of the ballads by Percy and Herder was a romantic construction centred in a notion of 'the people'. Perhaps what we need now is a new theoretical appraisal of 'the mind of the ballad poet', with equal regard to his social background in a feudal culture and to his implicit trans-formational grammar of epic, lyric and dramatic devices, using the advances of structuralist narrative theory from Propp onwards as already prefigured in the Danish folklorist Axel Olrik's sensational treatise on 'Epic Laws of Folk Poetry' (1908).

A much-debated phenomenological interpretation of the Danish ballads was given in 1959 by Villy Sørensen, one of the most brilliant minds in Denmark today, in an essay called 'Folkeviser og forlovelser' (Ballads and Engagements) in his collection of essays *Digtere og dæmoner* (Poets and Demons). Before R. D. Laing Villy Sørensen reads the ballads he selects as the living-through of an existential crisis, where love in the older type of ballad is an ethical redeeming power and in the younger an erotic reducing power, the outer demons of the Middle Ages settling in the interior of Renaissance man. Villy Sørensen uses Kierkegaard's concept of fear and Jung's arche-types to explain the view of the world of Medieval ballads. His reading is deliberately a-historic, but it need not be untrue, and at least he has made many younger readers see the ballads as relevant, living poetry.

This will be rather hard, I am afraid, for those who only read them in English. One of the 'official' translations (by E. M. Smith-Dampier, New York, 1939) contains stanzas like:

> *He led her to door of bridal bower*
> *That bride so bright of blee:*
> *'Hast thou forgot, proud Adelus,*
> *The troth thou didst plight to me?'*

– which sounds like Edgar Allan Poe with a hiccough. The Danish text, from the tragical story of Ebbe Skammelsøn, one of the greatest of the ballads, goes like this (in one version):

> *Ledte han den unge brud*
> *alt ad den højeloftsbro:*
> *'Og drages eder det til minde,*
> *I gav mig eders tro?'*
> *Fordi træder Ebbe Skammelsøn så mangen sti vild.*

(He led the young bride / All along the external gallery: / 'And is it drawn to your memory / you promised me your troth?' / Therefore Ebbe Skammelsøn threads so many a wild path.'). And then there are all the intricate repetitions of the surrounding stanzas. 'Ebbe Skammelsøn' is a tragical ballet about a lover, falsely reported dead, who comes home and kills his treacherous brother who stole his bride. So bright of blee, indeed! The poem is too good for poetasters.

It should be read not only as a tragic story of ethical realism, but also as a dance – best illustrated by the chalk paintings ('kalkmalerierne') on the walls of medieval Danish churches (the other great Danish contribution to medieval art), a sophisticated combination of dance, music, gesture, story-telling and poetry, a ritual singing game.

16

Renaissance, Humanism, Reformation

The sixteenth century was a period of intense intellectual activity in Denmark, where the great tendencies of Humanism, Lutheran Reformation and Renaissance often met in the same person. *Christiern Pedersen* (c. 1493, 1514, 1554), for instance, went to Paris to print dictionaries, and translated both Aesop and the New Testament (in 1524). The official translation of the whole Bible, the Danish King James Version, is Christian the Third's Bible from 1550. This is an important document of the Danish language, as is the Hymnal of 1569. Among the paraphernalia of the Protestant Reformation, the most amusing is the *Visitatsbog* (Visitation Book) of the bishop *Peder Palladius* (1503, 1537, 1560), not published until 1867. The first poet of note is *Hans Christensen Sthen* (1544, 1578, 1610) with some lovely hymns, brittle as a harpsichord. Sthen also contributed to school drama, that strange mixture of medieval moralities and Renaissance imitations of Seneca and Plautus, which flourished in Denmark between 1560 and 1630. These plays were written by provincial schoolmasters to be acted by their pupils. The liveliest is the crude farce *Karrig Nidding* (Niggard Knave) by *Hieronymus Justesen Ranch* (1539, 1585, 1607), which has been revived on stage in our day, and is a naive and funny moral story, enjoyable as long as you forget that it is contemporary with Shakespeare. Denmark was a little behind.

The Baroque

In the Baroque century, however, we really got up-to-date with the latest European – i.e. mostly German – literary fashions. The defence and illustration of the Danish language was led theoretically by *Peder Syv* (1631, 1663, 1702) and practically by *Anders Arrebo* (1587, 1611, 1637) with metrical translations of the Psalms (1623) and an epic poem, *Hexa-ëmeron* (published 1661). This was a free version of du Bartas' La Semaine, the typical Renaissance encyclopedic epic, which was adopted in many countries, e. g. by Arrebo's American contemporary Anne Bradstreet.

The modern revaluation of the Baroque which started in Germany before the First World War and in England shortly after with the revival of the 'metaphysical' poets has not yet quite penetrated Danish academic criticism. In Denmark one still finds an old-fashioned almost morally offended depreciation of the bombastic, 'unnatural' Baroque style. Apart from Kingo, the greatest poet of the period, it is only in recent years that the editing of Baroque texts has started. Here is certainly an example of that time-lag of forty years behind Europe, which some critics have suggested is a general characteristic of Danish culture ... Anyway, we have not had a Grierson and certainly no T. S. Eliot.

Nevertheless, we do have a Baroque poetry of note, though little drama and no novels. Here, too, a suspension of disbelief is necessary, not so much because of the metaphysical style, which the New Critics have taught us to appreciate, as because of the uncommon genres. Most of the non-religious Baroque poetry is occasional: poems for births and marriages and funerals, petitions, polemics and tributes to kings and noblemen. The religious poetry we have even less unimpeded access to. Its autocratic God is a mirroring of the autocratic monarch from the tributary poems, while the prostrate sinner mirrors the subject of absolute power of the political poetry. But as soon as one has experienced the enormous tension between chaos and order, which is the universal pattern in Baroque literature – which *is* the Baroque, in fact – it becomes possible to re-live this poetry.

Anders Bording (1619, published 1735, 1677) is the most easily accessible Baroque poet with charming erotic poems, drinking songs and humorous petitions. He also wrote the

Thomas Kingo.

first Danish newspaper, the monthly *Den danske Mercurius* (1666–77), reporting the news in stately Baroque alexandrines. *Søren Terkelsen* (?, 1645, 1656?) translated Opitz and Cats and (from German) Honoré d'Urfé's pastoral novel, *Astrée*, the success of which led him to publish some collections of his own charming pastoral poetry, *Astreæ Sjungekor* (Astrea's Singing Choir) (1648–54). The most mannered Baroque poet was *Elias Naur* (1650, 1683, 1728), whose *Golgotha paa Parnasso* (Calvary on Parnassus) (1689) is an ecstatic epic poem on the Passion.

The only truly great poet of the century was *Thomas Kingo* (1634, 1665, 1703) who excelled in all the Baroque occasional genres and also wrote a few lovely and passionate pastoral poems to his wives. But Kingo's greatest achievement is his hymns, published in *Aandeligt Siunge-Koor* (Spiritual Singing Choir) (1674–81) and in *Vinterparten* (The Winter Part) in 1689, a rejected proposal for a new hymnal. The Singing Choir, to tunes from Terkelsen's pastoral songs, is a week's family prayers: morning songs, evening songs and penitential hymns after David. In the later editions he added the shorter Morning Sighs and Evening Sighs. The second part has twenty hymns and twenty Heart Sighs. The hymnal contains revisions of older hymns, translations and new original poems. Kingo received a royal privilege on his hymnbook, but it was recalled a month later, because he had been too liberal in the selection of his own poems. A committee was set up, and in the official new hymnbook of 1699 Kingo had a hundred hymns included, and he was given the privilege of the new book for ten years.

It is an undeniable but never sufficiently explained fact that some of the greatest Danish poetry has been written for use in church – Kingo's in the seventeenth, Brorson's in the eighteenth, and Grundtvig's and Ingemann's in the nineteenth centuries. Whereas the churchsong of most other countries is usually, at best, second-rate poetry, we cannot leave the Danish hymns to the minor science of hymnology. They are poetry. Besides fulfilling the three functions of Baroque religious poetry which Helen Gardner (in her introduction to the Penguin Book of Metaphysical Poetry) describes as 'prayer, praise and meditation' – actually the three functions common to all religious poetry, not only Christian, and which one is sometimes tempted to think might be characteristic of all poetry – the poems designed for use in church fulfil a communal function. When they say 'we' they speak with the force of the actual congregation, and that is felt in every line of them. And they still speak. The hymns of Kingo and the later poets are still used in schools and in church services, though unfortunately often in shortened and mutilated versions.

Kingo's majestic rhetoric is gilded like a Baroque altar, as when he begins an Easter hymn:

Som den gyldne sol frembryder
gennem den kulsorte sky,
og sin stråle-glans udskyder,
  så at mørk og mulm må fly,
så min Jesus af sin grav
og det dybe dødsens hav
  opstod ærefuld af døde,
  imod påske morgen-røde.

(As the golden sun breaks forth / through the coalblack cloud / and its radiance discharges / so that dark and gloom must flee / so my Jesus from his grave / and the deep ocean of death / arose with honour from the dead / towards the Easter morning-red). The sunrise and the resurrected God are interchangeable in the poetic logic of the Baroque universe, and both are objects of prayer, praise and meditation.

Kingo's two most famous poems are 'Ked af verden og kær i himlen' (Tired of the world and enamoured of heaven) with the refrain 'Forfængelighed, forfængelighed' (Vanity) which changes in the middle of the poem to 'I Abrahams skød, / I Abrahams skød' (In Abraham's bosom), and 'Hver har sin skæbne' (Each has his destiny – there is an acceptable translation in Mitchell's anthology). They are tremendous emblematic structures expressing both the Baroque dialectics of here and beyond, of chaos and order, and universal human emotions.

How this chaos and this order filled the daily life of seventeenth century man can be seen from the greatest prose document of the period, the *Jammers Minde* (Memoir of Misery) by *Leonora Christina Ulfeldt* (1621, published 1868, 1698), which is the story of her prison-life. She was a daughter of King Christian the Fourth and spent more than twenty years in prison for high treason. As a document Jammers Minde is comparable to Pepys' diary, and Leonora Christina is an infinitely more likeable person than Mr. Pepys.

The intricate pattern of chaos and order can also be seen in the life and works of *Niels Steensen* (Nicolaus Steno) (1638, 1662, 1686) who after epoch-making scientific discoveries in medicine and geology converted and became a German Catholic bishop. Steno hardly belongs to Danish literature, but he is one of the greatest personalities of the seventeenth century, the century of Descartes and Pascal.

The Eighteenth Century

The aesthetics of the new classicism is appropriately advocated at the turn of the century by *Tøger Reenberg* (1656, c. 1700, c. 1742) whose versified *Ars poetica* (1701) follows Boileau. But the Baroque style lived on till past the middle of the century and found its last flowering in the humorous occasional poetry of *Christian Frederik Wadskiær* (1713, 1743, 1779). His poems for marriages and funerals (most of them still not edited) use the whole apparatus of Baroque conceits and a lot of terrible puns, but he gives them a twist of Rococo elegance and often satirical implications that show affinity with Holberg's rationalistic satire. Wadskiær is sheer fun, also in his very self-conscious knowledge of his own anachronism.

Ludvig Holberg (1684, 1711, 1754) is the greatest Danish writer of the first part of the eighteenth century, he is our Molière, our Voltaire, our Pope and our Addison in one, and he is not even Danish! That, at any rate, is an old dispute which shall not be revived here. He was born in Norway (which was part of Denmark then), and the Norwegians have claimed him eagerly ever since. However, he lived in Denmark and wrote in Danish (and in Latin), and has been lucky

Ludvig Holberg.

LVDEWIG HOLBERG
FREY-HERR VON HOLBERG.
geb. 1684. *gest. d 24 Febr 1754*

enough – like Eliot and Auden – to find a place in anthologies and literary histories of two countries.

If this were a history of literary kinds, Holberg would also find a place in several different chapters. He himself talked about his 'poetiske raptus' (poetic frenzy) in the 1720'ies, and this was followed by what has been called a 'historical frenzy' in the thirties and a 'philosophical and moral frenzy' in the forties and fifties. Holberg as a historical writer in Danish and Latin need not concern us here – he was a historian by profession, and after his studies at Oxford 1706 to 1708 his first book was an *Introduction to the History of the European Countries (1711).* After being appointed professor of history in 1730 he wrote his History of Denmark and several other works. His moral and philosophical writings include the

23

Latin utopian satire *Nicolai Klimii iter subterraneum* (1741), an international bestseller which was translated into both Danish and English (as Journey to the World Underground) the following year, and his Spectator essays in *Moralske tanker* (Moral thoughts) (1744) as well as five volumes of *Epistler* (1748–54), more than five hundred miscellaneous essays about ethics, philosophy, religion, history, literature and daily life, often both charming and wise.

Holberg's poetical frenzy started with verse satires culminating in the humorous epic *Peder Paars* (1719–20), an alexandrine take-off of Virgil, modelled on Boileau's *Le Lutrin*. It is a jaunty satire on Danish society, with a Don Quixote-like hero, often very amusing, and containing most of the themes of his comedies.

Holberg is above all *the* classical Danish comedy-writer, whose best plays are still acted, particularly at the Royal Theatre in Copenhagen which claims an unbroken stylistic continuity from the first performances. Holberg wrote, like Molière, for specific actors of the first Danish professional theatre which opened in 1722 and had to close temporarily in 1728, as a result of pietism gaining ground in Denmark. In five years he produced twenty-seven comedies. (When the theatre reopened at the end of the forties he wrote six more, relatively unimportant plays). Holberg's comedies are a national treasure, and it is almost sacrilegious to confess that I do not find them very funny. Admittedly, in comparison with Molière, whom Holberg found too aristocratic, Holberg is rather provincial. His wit is cruder, and the tragic implications of some of Molière's masterpieces are missing, leaving Holberg's plays rather two- or even one-dimensional. The characterization of the secondary characters as petty-bourgeois commedia dell'arte figures is very perfunctory, the lovers especially lacking Molièrean elegance. But in all fairness it must be said that Holberg's best plays are rapid satirical entertainments, and his main characters in the character comedies are as lively as Ben Jonson's. The satire, of course, is against excess, for moderation, and it is totally unfair – but sometimes unavoidable – to see Holberg as a rather wooden and pernickety defender of cheap morality. *Den politiske kandestøber* (The Political Tinker) is a satire on amateur politicians. *Jean de France* and *Erasmus Montanus* attack young people who follow outlandish fashions or believe more in scientific studies than in common sense. *Jeppe på Bjerget* (Jeppe of the Hill), a version of the old story of the farmer turned king, is deservedly his most popular comedy and a real treasure for a great actor. Most of these have been translated into English, whereas *Barselstuen* (The Lying-in Room) is perhaps untranslatable: it is a good-natured revue of human types, mostly female, given with an enormous responsiveness to individual styles and (lack of) linguistic logic. To me it is his funniest and most original play.

Holberg was doubtlessly an important writer, and still is. He is read and he is acted. For many reasons, both personal and social, he could not be a Danish Molière. But he is a very Danish Holberg.

The eighteenth century is the century of Enlightenment, but also of several darknesses and lesser lights. Contemporary with Holberg were both Brorson's pietistic Christianity and Stub's sparkling Rococo arias. *Ambrosius Stub* (1705, published 1771, 1758) was a poor clerk and private tutor whose poetry was only collected after his death: epigrams, drinking songs, love poems and nature poems in the form of elegant arias. One of them, 'Den kedsom vinter gik sin gang' (Dull Winter Went Its Course) is a spring poem of the utmost grace, rightly famous as one of the peak experiences of Danish poetry.

Rococo elegance also characterizes the poetry of *Hans Adolph Brorson* (1694, 1732, 1764) with its varied rhythms and echo effects. Brorson was a hymn writer expressing the emotional ecstasy of pietistic sectarianism, with special emphasis on the wounds of Christ. Jesus as the bridegroom and the soul as the bride appear in erotic imagery which is somewhat hard to swallow. But Brorson is also an eminent artist, and his best hymns are part of a living tradition. Often he attains the sublime, as in the Rococo painting of the created world in 'Op! al den ting' which begins:

> *Op! al den ting, som Gud har gjort,*
> *Hans herlighed at prise,*
> *det mindste han har skabt er stort*
> *og kan hans magt bevise.*

> *Gik alle konger frem på rad*
> *i deres magt og vælde,*
> *de magted' ej det mindste blad*
> *at sætte på en nælde.*

(Up! Every thing that God has made, / His glory for to praise, / the smallest thing he created is great / and can his power prove. // If all the kings went in a row / with their force and might, / They could not put the smallest leaf / on to a nettle again).

The Evangelical Christianity of the pietists prepared the way for the exaltation of the new poetry after 1750. Klopstock, the German poet, who wrote exalted odes in free rhythms lived for some years in Copenhagen and was, with Thomson and the other British nature poets, a great influence on some of the minor poets of the fifties and sixties and on Ewald in the seventies.

At the same time the satirical rationalism of Holberg lived on and found new exponents among the younger poets, especially in the Norwegian Society, the club of the Norwegian students in Copenhagen, where both emotional descriptive poetry and improvised epigrams and drinking songs were cultivated. The only important poet in this group was *Johan*

Hans Adolph Brorson.

Herman Wessel (1742, 1772, 1785). He wrote anecdotes in verse in the style of La Fontaine and one of the funniest comedies in Danish, *Kærlighed uden strømper* (Love Without Stockings) (1772), an absurd parody of the absurd Danish imitations of classical French tragedy, where everybody sings arias, says Ha! and dies in the end.

Johannes Ewald (1743, 1764, 1781) also made his characters say Ha!, but in earnest, and as he is one of our greatest poets he could do it. In his short life Ewald followed many influences, from Voltaire to Shakespeare. He tried his hand at all the kinds of literature which a professional writer might express himself in, from Spectator essays to national tragedy. His dramas – the Cornelian and Miltonic *Adam og Eva*, the

Nordic and Shakespearean *Rolf Krake* and the lovely operatic *Balders død* (Death of Balder) – are neither read nor acted now; only the realistic ballad opera *Fiskerne* (The Fishermen) has been revived, principally because it contains the Danish Royal Anthem, the magnificent 'Kong Christian stod ved højen mast' (King Christian stood at the high mast), which Longfellow translated.

Ewald still lives, however, as the writer of a handful of great poems and an autobiography which contains the liveliest Danish prose ever written. In many ways he belongs to what the Germans call Storm-and-Stress, the highly emotional, somewhat adolescent movement of the 1770'ies in most European countries, the greatest achievement of which was the American revolution.

The emotional breakthrough that happens in Ewald's poetry is the beginning of modern poetry, the ruthlessly private expression of personal experience. Ewald still wrote occasional poetry for money – he had to – of all the types established since the Renaissance, but he did it with a new emotional engagement, a new music, as in the Mourning Cantata for King Frederik the Fifth in 1766, one of his first great successes. (Ewald's connection with music and his collaboration with contemporary composers has never been investigated). It is always a new *music* which heralds a new period in literature, a new sound, a new way of handling language. Ewald is the Rousseau of Danish poetry. His great odes – principally 'Rungsteds lyksaligheder' (Beatitudes of Rungsted), 'Til min M' (To My M) and 'Til Sielen' (To the Soul) – are the first personal poetry in the modern sense. ('Ode to the Soul' is in Mitchell's anthology in an excellent translation).

In the same way *Levnet og Meeninger* (Life and Opinions) inaugurates modern prose. This 'autobiographical fragment' in the manner of Sterne, which was published posthumously in 1804, is in my opinion neither autobiography nor a fragment, but a deliberately fragmented piece of fiction, a short

Johannes Ewald.

poetical novel, which uses Ewald's early life as a pattern. Whatever it is, it is the most vivid and most beautiful of 'contributions to the knowledge of the human heart' (Ewald's own description of the book).

In the 1780'ies and 1790'ies the emotional revolution became either sentimentalism, political revolution or both. Clublife and the editing of magazines were the preoccupations of *Knud Lyne Rahbek* (1760, 1782, 1830), the first Danish professor of aesthetics, whose house in Copenhagen, Bakkehuset, is now a museum of that period which saw the beginning of Romanticism in Denmark. It was in a magazine, too, (in 1791–92) that *Johann Clemens Tode* (1736, 1782, 1806), a doctor and the Danish translator of Smollett, published his charming novel *Kierligheds nytte* (The Usefulness of Love) (in bookform 1803), the earliest Danish novel still readable today. The revolutionaries were people like *P. A. Heiberg* (1758, 1787, 1841) and *Malthe Conrad Bruun* (1775, 1795, 1826), both of whom were exiled for their radical satirical writings and spent the rest of their lives in Paris.

The great poet of the 1790'ies was *Jens Baggesen* (1764, 1785, 1826), and he paid dearly for his early success. When the new Romantic generation broke through with Oehlenschläger's sensational début in 1803 Baggesen became the scapegoat and was involved in endless polemics – and even lawsuits – with the new generation, which spoiled the rest of his life. And more than that, the 'Oehlenschläger school' established a dictatorship in the Danish literary world, which continues to be felt even today in the still inadequate and often unfair treatment of Baggesen. Attempts at revaluation have been made, mostly on the basis of his philosophical relations with Rousseau, Plotinus and the esoteric tradition. But Baggesen as a poet still awaits his rightful treatment. To do this we would need a rethinking of the periodization of the eighteenth and nineteenth centuries. This has already been attempted in England and America, but not in Denmark. If the period from 1750 til 1850 is seen as a unity, as a complicated pattern of tensions between emotion (Romanticism) and reason (Classicism, Neo-Classicism, Goethe's and the great Danish sculptor Thorvaldsen's), and without an abyss at the magical year 1800 – then the phenomenon Baggesen, too, could be seen as a unity. He is an extremely complicated poet, who perhaps reaches greater heights and depths than almost any other Danish writer. This can be seen in his complex and profuse poetry both in Danish and German and in his great prosework *Labyrinten* (The Labyrinth) (1792–93), an essayistic travelbook about art and existence, which is very famous though usually published in shortened versions. It is an enormously intense self-portrait, using Europe as a mir-

Jens Baggesen.

ror, a torrential prose-stream of laughter and tears, precise observations and aesthetic ideas.

Another beautiful loser of the nineties was *Adolph Wilhelm Schack von Staffeldt* (1769, 1804, 1826), our first Romantic poet, who printed his poems in magazines in Danish and German in the nineties, but only published his first book, *Digte* (Poems) one year after Oehlenschläger's, and unwisely predated some of them to try to prove his priority. Staffeldt did not have the pure, youthful genius of Oehlenschläger, but his philosophical odes and sonnets influenced by Kant and Schelling, Goethe and Schiller, are extremely interesting and often very good.

Both Baggesen and Staffeldt were extremists, in their personalities as well as politically and aesthetically. Perhaps the triumph of Oehlenschläger was the victory of Danish moderation over the extremists.

Romanticism

Adam Oehlenschläger (1779, 1802, 1850) was indeed a genius. One of the most famous anecdotes of Danish literary history tells of the young philosopher Henrik Steffens coming back from Germany to lecture at the university on the new German natural philosophy. He met Oehlenschläger and they had a sixteen-hour talk, after which Oehlenschläger rushed home and wrote 'Guldhornene' (The Golden Horns), the most famous poem in his first book *Digte 1803* (Poems 1803), published in December 1802, which introduced Romanticism into Danish literature. The golden horns, an art-treasure from the fifth century had just been stolen from the National Museum, but the poem is principally about the finding of the horns, one by a young girl, the other by a farmer, children of nature as against the rationalist scientists. Digte 1803 contains ballads, lyrical poems and a drama, 'Sanct Hansaften-spil' (A Midsummer Eve Play), which is an extremely lovely series of little scenes from a fairground, with satire of the bourgeoisie and much romantic love and visions of nature. It is all very summery and playful, ephemeral and eternal. Two and a half years later Oehlenschläger produced two volumes of *Poetiske skrifter* (Poetical Writings) (1805), containing cycles of lyrical poems, a prose saga, and the play 'Aladdin'. He has made this wonderful recreation of the Arabian Nights tale very Danish and Romantic. Aladdin is the young Romantic genius, to whom everything is given – a self-portrait of course – as opposed to the dark magician Noureddin (alias Baggesen). 'Aladdin' is not a dramatic masterpiece, and it is much too wordy, but it is the Romantic drama par excellence in Denmark – the closest parallel being Goethe's

Adam Oehlenschläger.

Faust – and has contributed a great deal to the national character which it depicts.

Oehlenschläger's third book, *Nordiske digte* (Nordic Poems) (1807) contains an epic poem and two tragedies, all of them with themes from Scandinavian mythology and ancient history. One of the tragedies, 'Hakon Jarl hin Rige' (Earl Hakon the Mighty. Excerpts in Mitchell's anthology) is a moving and impressive play. But after this Oehlenschläger lost his power. None of his works of the next thirty-five years fulfils his early promise, although there are some good lyrical poems, and the ballad tragedy *Axel og Valborg* (1810) and the cycle of romances *Helge* (1814) are good efforts. Oehlenschläger was *the* national poet. He was crowned with laurels in Sweden as the supreme poet of Scandinavia, but he had done his best work before he was thirty. Perhaps the reason was that his theme was youth. He is , as we shall see, not the last Danish poet tragically (or tragi-comically) to outlive himself.

The next generation of poets, recognizing Oehlenschläger as their master, chose other models than he. Instead of Goethe, Schiller and Nordic mythology they followed in their first period the German High Romantics. They were very ethereal, but changing with their times they changed to prose, following Walter Scott's example in the twenties and thirties. This goes for *Bernhard Severin Ingemann* (1789, 1811, 1862) and *Carsten Hauch* (1790, 1816, 1872), both prolific writers of dramas, novels and poetry. Ingemann's plays are insignificant, but Hauch's Shakespearean dramas are interesting. Hauch's novels are readable – with patience – *Guldmageren* (The Alchemist) (1836), *En polsk familie* (A Polish Family) (1839), a contemporary 'political' novel, *Robert Fulton* (1853) about the inventor, and others. Ingemann directly followed Scott in his four novels of the Danish Middle Ages, beginning with *Valdemar Seier* (1826), immensely lively historical panoramas of Danish history, which were a great success and have survived in shortened versions as children's books. But it was as lyrical poets that both Hauch and Ingemann excelled. Hauch did not publish his collected poems until 1842, and in this and his two later books there are some extremely good poems, principally odes in free verse in the style of Goethe. Ingemann wrote a great deal of interesting poetry and some very good short stories, but his fame rests on his hymns, especially the series of Morning and Evening Songs for Children which he wrote (1837–38) for the State Orphanage. They are simple, very beautiful songs about day and night, nature and God, with an unproblematical piety and a Blakean simplicity.

However, the greatest poet of the Romantic period is without doubt *Nicolai Frederik Severin Grundtvig* (1783, 1808, 1872). Whereas 'Kierkegaard' can be exported anywhere, it is

Nicolai Frederik
Severin Grundtvig.

almost impossible to make foreigners understand what the
phenomenon 'Grundtvig' is like. Perhaps because it has not
been sufficiently stressed that he is a great poet – in my opinion our greatest. At the centenary of his death a few years ago
no less than three books about him were published in English,
but none of them are likely to have reached people interested
in literature. In Denmark, too, Grundtvig has been taken
over by biographers, historians and theologians, not to speak
of mythomaniacs. There is material enough to employ all
these researchers for years to come. His collected works, if
they were published, would fill some three hundred volumes.
Grundtvig was a church reformer, preacher, historian, philo-
logist, pedagogue, politician, and visionary. But first and
foremost there is the wealth of his wonderful language: from

his earliest prose in *Nordens Mythologi* (1808, and a totally different version in 1832) to his last sermon, and in the proliferation of personal poetry about love, family, nature, country, sometimes devoloping into long, inspired visions like *Nyaars-Morgen* (New Year's Morning) (1824), in which he not just writes about Old Norse mythology, but lives it. I think it is Grundtvig's total identification which makes him the great poet he is, possessed both by his subject and by language. Perhaps, too, possessed by God in his Song Work.

Sang-Værk til den Danske Kirke (Song Work for the Danish Church (1837–1880), five volumes, the last three posthumous) is Grundtvig's collected hymns, 1500 poems, half of which are original, the rest masterly translations from several languages or re-workings of older Danish hymns. The Song-Work belongs to the Danish church, about 250 of the hymns are in the official hymnbook of the state church. But it also belongs to Danish poetry. Grundtvig preaches a message, he is concerned with theology, but he cannot help making it great poetry. The dialectical structure of the hymns, the prophetic truth of the rhymes, the whole Christian metaphorical emblematics united with homely images and God's grandeur in nature – all this, and wit. Grundtvig is a terrific punster, even in his hymns – it must be part of the diagnosis of his schizophrenia, I am sure – and there are seven times seven types of ambiguity in what he himself, with a characteristic play on words, called 'my indi-wit-duality'. As a young man he defined poetry as 'en sammensmeltning af syn og sang' (an amalgamation of vision and song). He is not only our Christian Emerson-and-Carlyle, he is one of the great visionary singers, like Wordsworth, Whitman and Yeats. Danish criticism still lacks a reading of Grundtvig's poetry using contemporary methods and contemporary feelings. It would need a Northrop Frye and a Harold Bloom.

I would like to give just one small example of Grundtvig's complex, overwhelming mastery, the first stanza of 'At sige verden ret farvel' from 1843–45, which is frequently sung at funerals:

> *At sige Verden ret Farvel*
> *I Livets Gry og Livets Kveld*
> *Er lige tungt at nemme;*
> *Det aldrig læres her paa Jord,*
> *Er, Jesus! ei Du i dit Ord,*
> *Hos os, som Du var hjemme!*

(To say farewell to the world aright / in life's dawn and life's evening / is equally heavy to learn; / it is never learned here on earth, / unless, Jesus! You are in Your word / with us, as if you were at home!). I shall not go into detail about this stanza (which is followed by five more, equally rich in poetry) and the syntactical dramas performed in it – the irony of the first three lines seeming to be a statement and then, by the semicolon, (a symbolical punctuation!) changed into an invocation, or the present indicative in line six where the subjunctive 'var' (were) would be correct grammatically, but not in the mytho-poetical logic. Let it suffice to point out the fantastic ambiguity in the last two lines: the idiomatic expression 'lad som om du er hjemme' (be as if you are at home, i.e. make yourself at home) is used to express the transsubstantiation of the Word in the present tense indicative. The combination of idiomatic expression and grammatical and syntactical ambiguity is characteristic of Grundtvig's mastery. (It is, by the way, found in Emerson, too, Grundtvig's soulmate, but with much less poetical force.)

Steen Steensen Blicher (1782, 1807, 1848) began as a preromantic with translations and imitations of Ossian, and never really got involved with the Romantic ideology. His best poems describe his regional Jutland, e. g. the cycle of beautiful poems *Trækfuglene* (The Migratory Birds) (1838) and the classic dialect collection *E Bindstouw* (1842) which makes

Blicher the Danish Burns. The latter is a series of stories and poems recited by Jutland farmers as an evening entertainment while knitting stockings. Blicher's greatest achievement, his short stories from 1824 onwards, could also be called regional literature, if that does not imply a limitation. He wrote them for provincial magazines for money, but they have survived as stories of quietly tragic, psychological realism, comparable to those of his younger Austrian contemporary Stifter. The same realism, but in an ironic, sophomoric version, characterizes *En dansk students eventyr* (Adventures of a Danish student) (1823–24, published 1843), the long fragment of a novel by *Poul Martin Møller* (1794, 1837, 1838), a philosopher who left mainly fragments, brilliant fragments in verse and prose, some of them philosophically anticipating Kierkegaard who admired him. The novelistic fragment is a witty psychological interpretation of human types with implicit Goethean criticism of Romantic excesses, which Møller also took up in a psychological thesis on 'affectation'.

The 'poetic realism' of the twenties had a parallel in the more aesthetic, often satirical cooled-down Romanticism in this and the following decade, often called 'Romantistic' and with Byron as its idol. The leading writer is *Johan Ludvig Heiberg* (1791, 1813, 1860), a learned Hegelian critic who supplied the Royal Theatre, of which he became the manager, with dramatic works of many types, the most popular being the so-called 'vaudevilles', witty, stylized entertainments with songs. The most famous of these is *Aprilsnarrene* (April Fools) (1826). Another of his plays, *Elverhøj* (The Elfin Hill) (1828) has become the classical national festival play. His later, more philosophical plays include *En sjæl efter døden* (A Soul After Death) (1841), a bitter anti-bourgeois satire. Heiberg's wife, *Johanne Luise Heiberg* (1812, 1848, 1890) who was the leading actress of the period, wrote her *Et liv, gjenoplevet i erindringen* (A Life Re-Experienced in Me-

Steen Steensen Blicher.

mory) (published 1891–92), the most famous memoirs of the nineteenth century, and a very rich and shrewd book. Heiberg's mother, *Thomasine Gyllembourg* (1773, 1828, 1856) also contributed to literature, pseudonymously, beginning with *En Hverdagshistorie* (An Everyday Story), a long series of penetrating stories of female psychology.

To Heiberg's circle belonged other clever and somewhat facile writers such as the poet and playwright *Henrik Hertz* (1797, 1827, 1870), the 'Victorian' erotic poet *Christian Winther* (1796, 1828, 1876) whose verse novel *Hjortens flugt* (The Flight of the Deer) (1855) has been extremely popular up till recent times, and the excellent Dionysiac poet *Ludvig Bødtcher* (1793, 1856, 1874) with a very scant production.

But the greatest new writer of the 1830'ies was *H. C. Andersen* (1805, 1829, 1875) – the Hans Andersen of children all over the world, most of whom do not even know that he is both Danish and literature. Andersen as the teller of nursery stories is a kind of joke to Danes, the only people to be able to appreciate his wit and his wisdom! Andersen was enormously productive in all literary genres, bad plays, sentimental poems, charming but flawed novels, brilliant journalistic travel sketches and memoirs – all of them about himself. He must have been an impossible person, a hypochondriac and egomaniac, sponging on his noble friends, always whimpering about lack of recognition or boasting of his fame. But his humour, his understanding and his language are miraculous. And when in 1835 he published his first collection of *Eventyr, fortalte for børn* (Fairy Tales, Told for Children) he found his niche. Andersen's 156 fairy tales and stories are of many sorts, from folktales and legends to deeply original myths, which are intended more for parents than for children. Andersen's stories are, of course, the most translated work of Danish literature. Yet they are untranslatable. One has to learn Danish to appreciate them.

And then you will be able to read Kierkegaard, too! *Søren Kierkegaard* (1813, 1838, 1855) is the famous Existentialist philosopher, but he is also a poet of Danish prose, a great poet who handles his philosophical syntax with unbelievable elegance. His great pseudonymous books are novels of a sort, experimental prose works with fictional personae, that can – and should – be read as literature. His last series of pamphlets against the official church, *Øjeblikket* (The Moment) (1855) are satires of unforgettable brilliance and scathing wit.

Here is the beginning af Andersen's 'The Ugly Duckling' (1842) with an attempt at a literal translation:

Der var så deiligt ude paa Landet; det var Sommer! Kornet stod guult, Havren var grøn, Høet var reist i Stakke

Hans Christian Andersen.

nede i de grønne Enge, og der gik Storken paa sine lan-
ge, røde Been og snakkede ægyptisk, for det Sprog havde
han lært af sin Moder. Rundtom Ager og Eng var der
store Skove, og midt i Skovene dybe Søer; jo, der var rig-
tignok deiligt derude paa Landet.

(It was so pretty out in the country; it was summer! The corn
stood yellow, the oats green, the hay was put up in stacks
down in the green meadows, and there the stork walked on
his long, red legs, talking Egyptian, for that language he had
been taught by his mother. Around field and meadow were
great woods, and in the middle of the woods deep lakes; yes,
it was really pretty out there in the country).

And here is Kierkegaard, from the preface to the first of his
Moment-pamphlets (also as literally as possible):

41

Saaledes er jeg et Menneske, om hvem det med Sand-
hed gjælder, at han ikke har den mindste Lyst til at virke
i Øieblikket – formodenligen er jeg just af den Grund
udseet dertil.

Naar jeg skal virke i Øieblikket, maa jeg, ak, tage Af-
sked med Dig, Du elskte Fjernhed, hvor der var Intet at
haste efter, altid god Tid, hvor jeg kunde vente Timer,
Dage, Uger for at finde Udtrykket just som jeg vilde ha-
ve det, medens der nu maa brydes med alle slige den
kjælne Forelskelses Hensyn. Og naar jeg skal virke i Øie-
blikket, vil der være en Deel Mennesker, hvem jeg skyl-
der det, dog idetmindste stundom at tage noget Hensyn
til alt det Ubetydelige, som Middelmaadigheden med
stor Vigtighed belærende foredrager, alt det Galima-
thias den, ved selv at bringe det med, faaer ud af hvad
jeg skriver, al den Løgn og Bagvaskelse, som et Menne-
ske er udsat for, mod hvem de to store Magter i Samfun-
det: Misundelse og Dumhed med en vis Nødvendighed
maa sammensværge.

Hvorfor vil jeg da virke i Øieblikket? Jeg vil det, fordi
jeg evigt vilde fortryde at lade det være, og evigt fortry-
de, om jeg lod mig afskrække ved, at den Slægt som nu
lever, vel i det Høieste kun vil kunne finde en sand Frem-
stilling af hvad Christendom er, interessant og mærke-
lig, for saa ganske roligt at blive hvor den er, i den Ind-
bildning at være Christne, og at Præsternes Legen-Chri-
stendom er Christendom.

(Thus I am a man about whom it can truly be said that he is
not in the least inclined to work in the Moment – presumably
that is just the reason why I have been designated to do it.

When I have to work in the Moment, then, alas, I must
take leave of thee, beloved Distance, where there was nothing to hurry about, always plenty of time, where I could wait
for days, hours, weeks to find the expression just as I wanted

42

Søren Kierkegaard.

it, while now all such considerations of mawkish infatuation must be broken with. And when I have to work in the Moment, there will be some people to whom I owe it sometimes at least to show some consideration for all the trivia that mediocrity with great importance didactically pontificates, all the tomfoolery that by bringing it itself it gets out of my writings, all the lies and slander a man must suffer against whom the two great forces in society, Envy and Folly, with sure necessity will conspire.

Why then do I want to work in the Moment? I want to, because I should eternally regret it if I did not, and eternally regret it if I let myself be put off by the fact that the generation now living would at most probably find a true account of what Christianity is interesting and strange, whereupon they would calmly remain as they are, imagining themselves to be Christians and the clergy, playing-at-Christianity, to be Christianity).

These two pieces of prose express the paratactical syntax of comedy and the hypotactical syntax of tragedy – each of them perfect and each of them life-giving.

While Andersen's international fame was immediate, it took Kierkegaard a hundred years to reach Europe and America. His contemporaries, of course, were impressed and a little shocked by his fury and his style, but they 'would calmly remain where they were'. Still, the moral seriousness of Kierkegaard can be felt in other writers of the forties – or a hedonistic reaction against it! *Frederik Paludan-Müller* (1809, 1833, 1876) started as a Byronic cynic and an elegant versifier, but his masterpiece *Adam Homo* (1841–48) is a very serious satirical verse novel in ottava rima, in the same sphere as Don Juan, Goethe's Wilhelm Meister and Dante's Commedia. Paludan-Müller's anti-hero gets on in the world but loses his soul and is only saved after death by the pure Christian love of the woman he forsook. Adam Homo is one of those masterpieces which it is a bit hard to love, I think, but it is very impressive and immensely clever.

Emil Aarestrup (1800, 1838, 1856) on the other hand it is very hard not to love. He is a great erotic poet, a big, fat provincial doctor who wrote a lot of short 'erotic situations', as he called them, with Heine as his model. But Aarestrup is better than Heine. Very often in the hedonistic playfulness a deep despair surfaces, which is not Byronic fashion but sincere understanding of life's basic phenomena. Although the fat country doctor and the New England spinster would seem to have very little in common, the closest parallel I can find to Aarestrup is Emily Dickinson. – She has the same precision, wit and fragility.

The ethical and religious tension of the 1840'ies also marked *Meïr Aron Goldschmidt* (1819, 1845, 1887) who

Emil Aarestrup.

started out as a journalist with deadly satirical attacks on
Kierkegaard, but who himself in a series of heavy but important novels moved close to a personal religion of fate, a
Nemesis-belief. Goldschmidt's novels are the first Danish
novels of international stature, and he seemed to think so
himself, too, for he moved to England and published some of
the books in his own translations, but nothing came of it. In a
way he is a Danish George Eliot, and his novels and stories
are still very much alive and readable. But the greatest novel
of the late Romantic period, in many ways ahead of its time
and still shocking in its psychological penetration is *Phantasterne* (The Fantasts) (1859), the only novel (apart from a
posthumous fragment) by the politician *Hans Egede Schack*
(1820, 1849, 1859). Phantasterne is an analysis of adolescent

imagination and its consequences in later life, a sort of final negation of the Romantic movement.

Modernism

I use the term Modernism for the period from about 1850–1870 and up to the present. I am quite sure that this term is just as useful (and just as indefinable – criticism is not a science of definitions!) as e. g. Baroque and Romanticism. And I am equally sure that it covers the literature of a well-defined period which is not yet over – or if it is we do not know it: one never knows till later when a new period has started. (Which means that I find the American term 'post-Modernism' modish and useless).

I see Modernism as divisible into the following periods:

1850–1880 The Forerunners (contemporary with late Romanticism/Victorian literature), the great inaugurators in France (Baudelaire, Flaubert) and America (Whitman, Dickinson) and isolated figures in other countries (such as Norwid in Poland and Hopkins in England).

1870–1900 Naturalism/Impressionism/Symbolism. The main point is not to give one decade to each -ism, as is usual in Danish literary history, but to remember that Mallarmé and Zola were contemporaries and friends. Naturalism and Symbolism are parallel methods af stylization, with Impressionism as a flutter or haze in between, and often the three -isms meet in the same writer.

1900–1930 The Many Isms (that is, 1900–1915 Art Nouveau and Expressionism, 1915–25 Futurism, Dada, Imagism, Vorticism, etcetera, 1925–1935 Surrealism, Vitalism and 'Neue Sachlichkeit' (Factionalism, Functionalism, Social Documentarism, etcetera)).

After 1930 I find a pattern af repetition, which seems to have an almost biological determinancy, as if at 25 every new generation of young writers took up what their fathers had discarded when *they* were 17 ... At all events, the thirties repeat the eighties, the forties took up the Symbolistic-Romantic preoccupations of the nineties, the fifties repeated the breakthrough of the new century and Expressionism, the sixties experimented once again like the Futurists and Dadaists, and in the seventies we have had both a Surrealistic (psychedelic) revival and a new social-political literature taking up where (or what) the thirties left off.

I know of course that this is too neat to be true, and I also know that the greater the author the more he contradicts the neat pattern. But the general scheme looks right to me, and it is useful. It should be emphasized, though, that this is the international development (as I see it), and that Denmark like other small countries does not often live up to it, either because we have been a downright backward country or because we do not have sufficiently important writers to fill out all the blanks. Nevertheless I shall proceed chronologically through modern Danish literature, and the closer we get to our own time the heavier becomes the critical responsibility of choosing some writers end skipping others, who may be important historically and on a local level, but need not concern foreign readers. A few writers who started publishing before the First World War or between the wars I shall just indicate the chronological position of in the following chapters in order to return to them in the final section about the years after 1945, when they wrote their most important books.

Naturalism, Impressionism, Symbolism

We started grandly. In the last thirty years of the 19th century three or four Danish writers – the critic Georg Brandes and the novelists Jacobsen and Bang and the now totally forgotten

47

(but once Nobel prize-winning) *Karl Gjellerup* (1857, 1878, 1919) – were famous in all Europe and especially in Germany, together with the other members of the 'Nordic Renaissance', primarily Ibsen from Norway and Strindberg from Sweden.

The beginning in Denmark was spectacular: the first lecture of *Georg Brandes* (1842, 1864, 1927) at the University as a guest lecturer on the third of November 1871: the beginning of his Main Currents in Nineteenth Century Literature, a new era proclaimed!

Brandes started as a Hegelian aesthetic critic, his first published book being a pamphlet against philosophical irrationalism. After a stay in Paris he changed his style and his method under the influence of Sainte-Beuve and Taine, but there is still a dialectical pattern in his six volumes of *Hovedstrømninger* (Main Currents) (published between 1872 and 1890): French, German and English literature in the first half of the century goes from revolution to reaction to a synthesis of liberalism. Brandes is not just writing literary history, he wants to influence the literature of his own backward country, and the purpose is clearly stated from the start: 'the proof that a literature in our time is alive is that it submits problems to debate'. Brandes was a radical, he was vehemently attacked by the conservatives, but he also had his followers and comrades in arms, and he *did* influence Danish literature. He changed it. But he himself changed, too. He spent some years in Berlin. When he returned to Copenhagen in 1882, the reactionaries were still in power, and Brandes in his bitterness found consolation in Nietzsche. He did not become a professor until 1902. Most of his later books are about great individuals – Voltaire, Goethe, Shakespeare, Caesar, Michelangelo – and use biographical methods (Shakespeare wrote forty plays, so if we know nothing about his life it is really our own fault, Brandes argued), not with the positivist indiscriminate finding of facts, but in a cool, balanced but emphatic process of

Georg Brandes.

identification. Brandes is a great critic, not because of his methods or his evaluations – both are dated – but because of his mind. It is still fascinating to read him, he demands our attention.

J. P. Jacobsen (1847, 1876, 1885) was the only genius among Brandes' Danish followers, but he was a rather unruly pupil. He was a botanist by profession, and translated Darwin. His scientific schooling governs his writing from the start, and in both his sensational début, the long short story *Mogens* (printed in a literary magazine in 1872) and in his two novels, *Fru Marie Grubbe* (1876) and *Niels Lyhne* (1881), the confrontation between the main character and a series of psychological types of the opposite sex follows a biological pattern, with desire and death as the driving forces in the individual. Niels Lyhne was always called 'the atheist's bible' in the days when atheism was something you really believed in. But the novels are more than a 'debate of problems', they are artefacts, and their minutely chiselled language is miraculously alive and moving. In his programme and in the 'biological' structure of the novels, Jacobsen is a Naturalist, but in details he is a Symbolist. Passage after passage from the books – not purple, but scarlet – can be taken out and admired, but can also be put back again and seen to belong to the structure. I know of no more *perfect* books in Danish literature, but the perfection has not congealed, it is so full of nervous agility. The same goes for Jacobsen's short stories and his few but marvellous poems, mostly published after his death, the first Modernist poetry in Denmark. Especially the free-verse poems Jacobsen called 'arabesques' (after Poe) with their mimetic metrics, are shockingly novel, and not just for their age. No wonder that Rilke (in the Malte-novel) and Arnold Schönberg (in his Gurre-Lieder) admired and used Jacobsen. He is still useful.

Holger Drachmann (1846, 1872, 1908) was the other important new writer of the seventies, but he is now largely – and partly unjustly – forgotten. He was an uncontrolled lyrical talent with Shelley and Byron (his translation of Don Juan equals the original) as his masters, and he has written beautiful lyrical poetry. He is one of those poets whose creative periods and ideological changes are closely connected with their private lives, and Danish literary history knows all about Drachmann's various wives. Of his enormous production of plays and novels the fairy-tale comedy *Der var engang* (Once Upon a Time) (1885) has been a permanent success on stage, and his formless but poetical novel *Forskrevet* (Pledged) (1890) is famous for its energetic descriptions of bohemian life. Drachmann's best prose is in his more unpretentious short stories, especially the simple dramatic tales of the life of fishermen. But first and last Drachmann is a lyrical poet, of-

J. P. Jacobsen.

ten with grand gestures that today seem rather ridiculous –
'min vin, min kårde og min elskerinde' (my wine, my sword,
and my mistress) – swashbuckling poetry, but often, too, poetry with a hauntingly euphonious and euphoric beauty in
great surging stanzas.

Herman Bang (1857, 1879, 1912) started as a brilliant journalist and literary critic, advocating Naturalism. But in his
own novels and short stories his biological determinism – his
inherited degeneration and his homosexuality – is transformed into a sparkling dramatic impressionism where everything happens in dialogue, in implications and innuendoes.
Bang wanted to be an actor, he became a theatre director –
e. g. putting on Ibsen for Lugné-Poe in Paris – and a famous
reader of his own works. He was harassed by society for his

'criminal' sexual inclinations, which partly explains his hypersensitive style, and also the enormous tension between a hopeless longing for love and an acceptance of desire as a biological fate which is his main theme. His ideas about 'the scenic novel' he practised with a breath-taking skill which makes him the Henrik Ibsen of the novel. In the novels and short stories which have made him famous the voice is everywhere an actor's voice, and every sentence abounds with sensitivity, suggestion and wit. His character portraits are full of compassion, but also drawn at the director's distance – the kind of moral feeling which makes 'putting up a good show' the greatest compliment. Bang's moral sensitivity can be compared to that of Henry James and Marcel Proust, while his mosaic of voices might remind a modern reader of Ivy Compton-Bur-

Henrik Pontoppidan.

nett's novels, but Bang is so utterly original that he ought to be given his rightful place in world literature once more. There is nobody like him.

Where Bang can be almost hysterically refined, *Gustav Wied* (1858, 1887, 1914) is terribly rough. The nihilistic satire of his novels, short stories and plays is desperate, and in between desperately funny. His most original innovation were his 'satyrspil' (satirical plays), closet dramas with more stage directions than dialogue. The pessimism of Bang and Wied was a direct consequence of the biological determinism of Naturalism, and this also applies to *Henrik Pontoppidan* (1857, 1881, 1943) though he was a much stronger character and has the saving moral vision of the great novelist. His three great panoramic novels *Det forjættede land* (The Promised Land) (1891–95), *Lykke-Per* (Lucky Per) (1898–1904) and *De dødes rige* (The Kingdom of the Dead) (1912–16) are both chronicles of fifty years of Danish society and Danish history, and ethical parables of individual development. The novels – and Pontoppidan's other novels and short stories – are immensely readable, both for their grand epic sweep and for their wealth of psychological shadings, showing the wise compassion of Pontoppidan even in the toughest satire.

If prose had dominated the eighties, the new generation of writers were poets. Their little magazine *Taarnet* (The Tower) (1893–94) was the organ of French Symbolism, but the young poets and painters gathering around it soon followed their own very different paths. *Viggo Stuckenberg* (1863, 1886, 1905) was a consistently stoic atheist in his fluent, moralistic verse. *Johannes Jørgensen* (1866, 1887, 1956) became a Catholic, and apart from his often serenely beautiful poetry is mostly known for his pious travel books, his biographies of saints and the story of his own conversion in *Mit livs legende* (The Legend of My Life) (1916–28). Jørgensen spent most of his life in Italy, and became famous there for his devotional writings.

Sophus Claussen (1865, 1887, 1931) is the great Danish Symbolist poet, our Yeats, only with eroticism taking the place of the spirits. The popular image of Claussen in his lifetime – though he did not become popular at all until the forties – was of a jovial hedonist who could write lovely poems about Danish nature, but who was often too difficult. He wrote charming prose – novels and travel sketches – and his two collections of essays, *Løvetandsfnug* (Dandelion Fluff) (1918) and *Forårstaler* (Spring Talks) (1927) contain criticism that is only comparable to Wallace Stevens' The Necessary Angel, and with the same ethos, the same absolute belief in the imagination. But it is with his six great collections of poetry – after the rather derivative first book in 1887 – that Claussen proves himself to be *the* great modern poet of Den-

Sophus Claussen.

mark: *Pilefløjter* (Willow Whistles) (1899), *Djævlerier* (Dev-ilries) (1904), *Danske vers* (Danish Verse) (1912), *Fabler* (1917), *Heroica* (1925) and *Hvededynger* (Heaps of Wheat) (1930).

To prove the case I shall quote one poem, 'Væk ikke sva-nerne' (Do not awaken the swans) from Fabler with a prose translation, whereby one misses the virtuoso perfection of the three-syllable rhymes, but can still follow the intricate rhe-torical pattern and the subtle implied negation of this multi-level poem about the necessity of the imagination:

> *Mit vårfløjt blev nedstemt af andedams-claquerne.*
> *Selv svanerne rystede svanenakkerne.*

Fjerhammene bruste, mens næppe de målte mig
med sideblikke, der lod, som de tålte mig.

En enkelt kom sagtelig sejlende hen:
Lig stille og ti, er du svanernes ven ...

Det er svane-skæbne, at alt må dræbe os,
livet er til for at efterstræbe os.

Kom ikke med trækfugletoner forlystende
til svanen, som drømmer sin isdrøm, den rystende ...

En brøde er livet, og vi – vi er sonerne,
kun født til at synge med døden i tonerne.

Men ildner du os med det hede og higende
– den dobbelte islæt i trækfugleskrigene –

og må vi ej blunde til solnedgangsklokkerne,
vi rejser os. Ve over livs-forlokkerne!

Vi rejser os. Fyrige svulmer da hammene.
I fald vi er stækkede – dø må vi flammende.

Ak, svanerne lokker man kun for at slæbe dem
i hobevis sammen ... og derefter dræbe dem.

Til evige vintre har stængt oceanerne
og snefald får mundene lukt på vulkanerne –

væk ikke, med ildhu og krigerisk dystende,
de vingefjer-brusende, kraftig sig brystende!

Lad festskrud og lege på drømmebanerne
forlyste de sorgfulde. Væk ikke svanerne!

(My spring whistling was voted down by the duckpond
    claques.
Even the swans shook their swans' necks.

56

The suits of feathers rustled, while they hardly measured
   me
with sidelong glances pretending to suffer me.

A single one came gently sailing up:
Lie still and be quiet, if you are a friend of the swans . . .

It is the swans' fate that everything must kill us,
life exists to persecute us.

Do not come with migratory birds' notes diverting
to the swan dreaming its ice-dream, the shivering . . .

An offence is life, and we – we are the atoners,
only born to sing with death in our notes.

But if you fire us with the heat and the craving
– the double train of the migratory birds' cries –

and if we are not allowed to doze to the sunset bells,
we rise. Woe to the life-seducers!

We rise. Fervently then the suits of feathers swell.
If we are clipped – we must die in flame.

Ah, swans are only decoyed to be hauled
together in great heaps . . . and then killed.

Until eternal winters have locked the oceans
and snowfall shuts up the mouths of the volcanoes –

do not awaken, with enthusiasm and warlike fighting
the wingfeather-rustling, the mightily strutting ones!

Let festival suits and games on the dreamtracks
entertain the sorrowful ones. Do not awaken the swans!)

This is only one moment in Claussen's great composite poem
about the life of the imagination, 'the heat and the craving',
the eroticizing of the universe through poetry – here illus-

trated proudly and with compassion by letting the other poets, the swans, argue their case.

Among the other poets of the Nineties were the efficient but rather hollow *Helge Rode* (1870, 1891, 1937) and the aristocratic nature poet *Ludvig Holstein* (1864, 1895, 1943). Rode's poems, plays and essays demonstrate a spiritualistic idealism which was based on a mystic experience. Holstein's first collection was published in 1895, his second twenty years later. He is a Danish 'Georgian' who writes beautiful, quiet poetry about nature and the eternal rhythm of life and death and recreation, perfect minor poetry.

The Regional Generation

Most of the important prose writers of the first two decades of this century published their first books in the nineties, often wildly Symbolist or Decadent experiments, before they changed their style and took part in 'det folkelige gennembrud' (the popular breakthrough) as it has been called to emphasize both the difference from the 'exclusiveness' of the nineties-writers and its continuation of Brandes' 'modern breakthrough' in the seventies. Another name given to these writers collectively was 'the Jutland movement'. Most of them came from Jutland, and they very consciously practised 'regional' literature, protesting against the decadence of the big city, Copenhagen. This also partly accounts for the uneasy clash between revolutionary intention and reactionary form: even the most Modernistic of these writers, Johannes V. Jensen, the world-traveller, had difficulty in reconciling his modernity with his home background.

At the same time, Freud was in the air. If Expressionism as a literary style did not really catch on in Denmark, at least not before the twenties, Expressionism as a life-style was everywhere present. The novel of individual psychology is an

Expressionist phenomenon. The most 'ninetyish' of the new writers was *Harald Kidde* (1878, 1900, 1918) whose *Aage og Else* (1902–03), *Helten* (The Hero) (1912) and the fragment *Jærnet* (The Iron) (1918) are Symbolist, rather mannered novels of carnal and spiritual psychology. The still much too neglected *Knud Hjortø* (1869, 1899, 1931) was also an eminent and rather mannered psychologist, especially in extremely sensitive and sympathetic short stories about women and children.

The propagandist novels about smallholders and tenant farmers by *Johan Skjoldborg* (1861, 1893, 1936) and *Jeppe Aakjær* (1866, 1899, 1930) were very popular and had a direct political effect, but are now forgotten. Aakjær, however, survives as a marvellously musical lyric poet, whose songs, often in dialect (and influenced by Burns) and often set to music by Carl Nielsen, the great composer of the period, are part of every Dane's heritage. Aakjær's first wife *Marie Bregendahl* (1867, 1904, 1940) wrote quietly intense novels about farmers, in sharp contrast to the sadistically moralizing novels of *Jakob Knudsen* (1858, 1887, 1917), an Old-Lutheran reformer whose prime message was: Love thy neighbour and thrash thy children. Knudsen is a directly offensive reactionary writer, but, admittedly, a good story-teller.

Just as tendentious and an even better story-teller is the communist *Martin Andersen Nexø* (1869, 1898, 1954), the most read Danish author east of the Iron Curtain. His two great proletarian novels *Pelle Erobreren* (Pelle the Conqueror) (1906–10) and *Ditte Menneskebarn* (Ditte Child of Man) (1917–21) are in the best sense popular novels, not just a demonstration of socialist realism, but attractive and moving works of art, as are many of Nexø's short stories and his memoirs. Also *Henri Nathansen* (1868, 1899, 1944) is in a way a 'regional' writer. His novels about Jewish business-men and petty bourgeois in Copenhagen are forgotten, but his play *Indenfor murene* (Inside the Walls) (1912) has become a much performed classic of the Danish theatre. It is the best Danish example of the after-Ibsen well-made play, a sentimental comedy about the conflicts, in a Jewish family, between old-fashioned ghetto mentality and the new capitalist society.

The greatest lyric poet of the 'Jutland movement' was *Thøger Larsen* (1875, 1895, 1928) whose combination of the local and the cosmic makes him an equal of contemporaries such as E. A. Robinson and Robert Frost. Larsen was a provincial newspaper editor and an amateur astronomer. His cosmic pantheism is entirely non-Christian, totally biological, and he finds wonderful expression for his double experience of transience and permanence. Larsen is a nature poet in a new sense, writing – as Olaf Bull, Norway's greatest modern poet, did at the same time – about the Nature of the new science. This permeates every stanza of lyrical description in Larsen's poetry and also his most famous poem, 'Jens Højby', a deeply moving portrait of a bed-ridden old farmer waiting for death and extinction.

Johannes V. Jensen (1873, 1896, 1950) is rightly the most celebrated writer of his generation. He received the Nobel Prize in 1944, but his permanent achievement is the explosion of books he gushed forth in the first ten years of the century: novels, short stories, essays, poems – he excelled in all genres and really brought something new into Danish literature. But like Oehlenschläger he spent the rest of his long life writing books that were not as good as those of his youth, and often simply dreadful. Both Jensen's glorification of 'health', his 'Gothic Renaissance' with England (imperialism) and America (technology) as the model nations, and his Darwinistic evolutionism and 'scientific' mythology are rather suspect today. Even his famous series of novels *Den lange rejse* (The Long Journey – i. e. from the Ice Age to Christopher Columbus, who was found to be typically Nordic) (1908–22) is almost unreadable today in spite of its brilliant style.

Johannes V. Jensen.

But what survives is quite a lot: the poetry, or rather the
four or five marvellously fresh Whitmanesque free-verse
poems in *Digte 1906* (Poems 1906), a new diction, a new
music and new themes; the subtle and genial regional tales in
the three collections of *Himmerlandshistorier* (Himmerland
Stories) (1898–1910); the best of his 'myths', the rather mean-
ingless but also very typical name he gave to the short stories,
essays, prose poems and travel sketches etcetera in a long
series of miscellaneous collections beginning with *Myter og
jagter* (Myths and Hunts) (1907); and his miracle of a historical novel *Kongens Fald* (The Fall of the King) (1900–01),
which I do not hesitate to call the best of all Danish novels.
Ideologically, Kongens Fald is a sort of summary of the pessimism of the nineties, but in its almost brutally beautiful

61

liveliness the style refutes the contents, or counterbalances it – the fall is the ideology but language is the king. It is a visionary novel, and in every sentence uses the vision of language to see the world. The 'breakthrough' around 1900, of which Jensen is the greatest representative, was a popular breakthrough also in the sense that it was a breakthrough of the senses. You hear, see, taste, smell and feel through Jensen's prose. And that of course is Expressionism, the turning inside out of Impressionism, the new physical psychology. Kongens Fald is a thrilling story but it is also a composite portrait of Denmark, of its psyche, its landscape, its weather. Just one short quotation:

> *Næste dag red de videre i klart, lyst aprilsvejr. Hestene knuste de blå pytter på vejen. Udenfor skovene strakte landet sig tyndt overgydt med en forårsfarve, man så milevidt hen i den nye luft. Langt borte lå runde gravhøje dristigt på de øverste landrygge, hvide af dug på den venstre side.*

> (The next day they rode on in clear, bright April weather. The horses crushed the blue puddles in the road. Beyond the woods the countryside stretched out, thinly suffused with a spring colour, you could see for miles through the new air. In the far distance round burial mounds lay daringly on the upper land-ridges, white with dew on their western side.)

To a Danish reader every word and every phrase is new in such a text – and still is 75 years after it was written. And hasn't it the same colours and the same forms that Matisse and Picasso were using in their paintings about that time? The little oddities in the vocabulary, the obliquities are deeply significant. You could see for miles 'hen i' the new air, it says. 'Hen i' means something like 'far away into': the reader can imagine the gazing of the riders, the dreamers.

Jensen has, of course, had an enormous influence on later Danish prose and poetry. His most immediate follower was *Albert Dam* (1880, 1906, 1972), who published two novels in 1906 and 1908 and then a third in 1934, but who only became well-known after his seventieth year – with his ten books published in the fifties and sixties he belongs in our next chapter. There we shall also meet another great storyteller, *Karen Blixen* (1885, 1934, 1962), known to the English-speaking world as *Isak Dinesen*. She published her first stories in literary magazines in 1907, but she seems not to belong to any special period in our literary history.

Very period, on the other hand, were most of the other writers who started publishing in the years around the First World War. *Kai Friis Møller* (1888, 1910, 1960) was a brilliantly witty reviewer and parodist, and as a translator of poetry he took on many different jobs, among them T. S. Eliot, but his own poetry is Art Nouveau or Jugendstil, thin and neatly decorated. Another virtuoso without anything very important to say was *Hans Hartvig Seedorff* (1892, 1916), the most popular new poet during and after the war, a miniature Drachmann. Among the prosewriters *Otto Rung* (1874, 1902, 1945) should be mentioned for his literary crime stories in the manner of Poe.

But the most original new writer was *Robert Storm Petersen* (1882, 1913, 1949), known to every Dane as *Storm P.*, our greatest humourist. For forty years he filled Danish newspapers and weeklies with wonderfully nonsensical drawings and texts, and he published a profusion of books, mostly collections of monologues, which he had usually first performed himself in cabarets – an enormous treasure of crazy humour, often with hidden social satire in it, but always full of the wildest linguistic inventions and imitations of Copenhagen slang. Storm P. was his own Expressionist and his own Dadaist, and he is utterly original. Indeed he ought to be known all over the world.

The Twenties and Thirties

The Danish Expressionist and Cubist painters had their own magazine, *Klingen* (The Sword Blade) (1917–20), in which the poets wrote, too, among them *Otto Gelsted* (1888, 1913, 1968). He should have been predisposed to be a Modernist, with his interests in both modern painting and Freud; but he was a classicist at heart, and in addition a communist, and he argued sharply against those new -isms in literature that he willingly accepted in painting. Most of Gelsted's poems are quiet, stoic nature lyrics, but he could also write free-verse satires on the modern mentality, like the revolutionary 'Reklameskibet' (The Show Boat) from 1923 about a young student who blows up modern civilization, and in the thirties scathing epigrams against nazis and reactionaries ('Strike out the ugly cross from our flag, / make it red!'). The most avant-garde writer was *Emil Bønnelycke* (1893, 1917, 1953), now totally forgotten, but once the great young hope & scandal, who while reading his prose poem about Rosa Luxembourg at a poetry reading fired a revolver, as a symbolic gesture.

Tom Kristensen (1893, 1920, 1974) also fired a gun: the poem 'Landet Atlantis' (That Land Atlantis) in his first book, *Fribytterdrømme* (Buccaneer Dreams) (1920) ends with the words:

> *I chaos jeg løfter min bøsse*
> *mod skønhedens stjerne og sigter.*

(In chaos I raise my gun / toward the star of beauty and take aim). And earlier in the same poem he declared:

> *Skøn som en sønderskudt banegård*
> *er vor ungdom, vor kraft, vore vilde ideer.*

(Beautiful as a railroad station shot asunder / is our youth, our power, are our wild ideas). This desperate new beauty of

Tom Kristensen.

chaos after the war is expressed by the young Tom Kristensen in his first three books of poetry and in two experimental novels, though the novels are not quite good enough and the poems are almost too good – their grand gestures and their Kiplingesque rhythms are a bit too overdone. Tom Kristensen was our best modern critic – a Danish Edmund Wilson – and he was the first to introduce the new modern writers, Kafka, Joyce, Lawrence. But he did not seem to have the sustaining power to lead a Modernist revolution in Danish literature. In a famous essay as early as 1925, 'Our modern poetry and its crisis', he took leave of the Modernist aesthetics: 'To confess that everything was beautiful was to stand unarmed'. What he wanted to stand armed against was anguish, existential fear – neither whisky nor rhythms and metaphors and colours could fight that. And that is exactly the theme of his masterpiece, the novel *Hærværk* (Havoc) (1930), the last important book he wrote. Tom Kristensen wrote beautiful poems before and after 1930, as well as essays, short stories and travel sketches – the travelbook *En kavaler i Spanien* (A Cavalier in Spain) (1926) is extremely good. But his supreme artistic achievement is Hærværk, a novel about the twenties, and about a special Copenhagen newspaper milieu (with scandalous portraits from life), but most of all it is a story about the existential fear of an alcoholic. No wonder that Tom Kristensen, the always perceptive critic, hailed Malcolm Lowry's Under the Volcano when it was translated into Danish. His own Hærværk is, like Lowry's book, a fever of abstinence and a fever of booze, a nervously realistic world turned into a nightmare of emptiness, a myth of the soul.

The other important novelist of the twenties was *Jacob Paludan* (1896, 1922, 1976), who declared himself from the start a reactionary against modern civilization, materialism, women's liberation etc. Paludan, too, was a very good critic and an excellent essayist, and he, too, did his most important work before he was forty: four novels in the twenties culminating in *Jørgen Stein* (1932–33), the best of the typical 'Bildungsromane' from the years between the wars, a good story about a young man's evolution and the society he lives in and at last flees from to find an unspoilt rural idyl and a wife. It is a clever and well-written traditional epic novel, but not exactly exciting.

In the twenties the new drama in Denmark began with three or four first-class playwrights. The oldest, *Sven Clausen* (1893, 1920, 1961) was a professor of law who wrote witty, rather dry comedies that are now, perhaps unfairly, neglected. *Soya* (1896, 1923) had his greatest success with his first comedy *Parasitterne* (The Parasites) in 1929, a cruel but very effective psychological study in the manner of the classical type comedies. His many later plays are often crude and superficial, but very successful is the Pirandello-inspired tetralogy *Blindebuk* (Blind Man's Buff) (1940–48) beginning with *Brudstykker af et mønster* (Fragments of a Pattern) where the point is that there *is* no pattern, everything is random, and ending with the satirical play *Frit valg* (Free Choice) where the point is, etcetera.

Equally sensational was *Kaj Munk* (1898, 1928, 1944), a polemical country parson whose first work was also his best, *En idealist* (An Idealist) (1928) a Shakespearean drama of ideas about Herod. Munk was murdered by the nazis as an outspoken supporter of the resistance movement, after some flirtation with Hitler in the thirties and dramas about 'great men'. His heroic death partly explains an enormous over-rating right after the war. But En idealist is a good play, and so is the Christian documentary about an awakening from the dead by faith, *Ordet* (The Word) (1932), filmed by Carl Th. Dreyer, our only filmmaker of international renown. Munk at his best, writing sensitive, tense dialogue, can be seen in the one-act play *Før Cannae* (Before Cannae) (1943), a discussion between Hannibal, the dictator and Fabius, the procrastinator (translated in Mitchell's anthology).

Beginning with a thundering success seems to be the rule with Danish dramatists. *Kjeld Abell* (1901, 1935, 1961), too, started well, with the Brechtian musical *Melodien, der blev væk* (The Melody That Got Lost) (1935), a little-man-what-now trifle of the thirties, very charming and very 'modern'. Abell's next success was very different but also very Brechtian: *Anna Sophie Hedvig* (1939), a political drama about the necessity of fighting evil, i.e. the nazis. Abell's first play after the war, *Silkeborg* (1946) was also a great success, an effective dramatization of the resistance movement contra the silent majority. But then his luck turned. All his later plays – though brilliantly performed at the Royal Theatre – were found too 'difficult', and one of them, *Vetsera blomstrer ikke for enhver* (Vetsera Does Not Blossom for Everyone) (1950) triggered off the first of those debates about 'obscurity in literature' that have characterized the official climate in Denmark since the war. Vetsera – which is a new version of the Mayerling-drama –, *Dage på en sky* (Days Upon a Cloud) (1947) and *Den blå pekingeser* (The Blue Pekingese) (1954) have the intellectual wit of Giraudoux and Anouilh, but also some of the visionary qualities of Strindberg, and I am sure that they (and Abell's marvellous prose writings) will be resurrected at the next turn of fashion's wheel and come back to stay.

Among the many important new poets of the twenties some practised local variations of the international -isms, while others were traditionalists or populists. A special case is *Paul La Cour* (1902, 1922, 1956), who discarded his first Modernist attempts. For most of the twenties La Cour lived in Paris, and his essays and translations show his intimate knowledge of modern art and literature, but his own poetry, in a series of large volumes up to 1940, is strangely sentimental and rhetorical in a bad sense. Not until after the war did he emerge as a modern poet, and I shall therefore return to him in my next chapter where we shall also meet *Jens August Schade* (1903, 1926, 1978), the greatest poet of the twenties and the liveliest force in modern Danish literature.

Some other poets of the period, some of them still writing, should be given honorable mention. Most of them contributed to the little magazine *Vild Hvede* (Wild Wheat), which still exists, now in its fifty-first year. Since 1951 it has been called *Hvedekorn* (Grains of Wheat) and I have the honour of being its present editor. It is still the place where most young Danish writers publish their first poems. *Johannes Weltzer* (1900, 1920, 1951) was a very minor poet who became famous for a Dadaistic sound poem. More substantial is *Johannes Wulff* (1902, 1928) who has steadily produced poems, lyrical novels and short stories with naive charm and obstinate individuality, defending cosmic consciousness and human compassion and friendliness.

Allan Bock (1890, 1928) in *Byen ved floden* (The City on the River) (1927) wrote Objectivist poetry with penetrating psychological wisdom, which also characterizes *Bogen om Ruth* (The Book of Ruth) (1955), a story in verse about a poet's love and inspiration, and the great and very original three-volume verse novel *Skrevet i mandtal* (And All Went to Be Taxed) (1968–74) about a large modern industrial firm, a milieu Bock knows from his own working life. The 'Neue Sachlichkeit' also characterizes *Poul Henningsen* (1894, 1928, 1967), editor of the Functionalist magazine *Kritisk revy* (1926 –29) and inventor of a lamp which is one of the triumphs of Danish design. PH (the initials he was known under) was a keen controversialist and, as a poet, wrote the best and most meaningful modern cabaret couplets we have, many of them deservedly classics, proving that 'brugskunst', too, (art for use, the Danish term for 'arts and crafts' and 'design') can be great art.

Among the traditionalists *Per Lange* (1901, 1926) is the classical poet, with few but exquisite poems in *Kaos og stjernen* (Chaos and the Star) (1926) and only two later collections. In the fifties and sixties he published some volumes of perfectly styled, but rather morose essays. He is remembered for six or eight perfect, marmoreal poems which in strict metres and complex metaphorical structures express the same chaotic beauty and its consequent pessimism as Tom Kristensen did. Lange's absolute contrast was *Nis Petersen* (1897, 1926, 1943), the most popular poet of the thirties and forties and totally unreadable for my generation and younger readers. He also had a great international success with his journalistic novel of ancient Rome, *Sandalmagernes gade* (The Street of the Sandalmakers) (1931). Petersen's poems are inflated rhetorical stunts about love and religion, liquor and vagabondage – his favourite poet was Robert W. Service – and it is almost impossible to understand today why thousands of readers were shaken by a pathetic fake like 'Brændende Europa' (Burning Europe) or 'Elsker du mennesket?' (Lovest thou man?) (translated in Mitchell's anthology). (But I suppose that we today have our own mawkish sentimentalists who will be taken down by the next generation).

An uneasy balance between hysterical emotionalism and real emotion was struck by *Hulda Lütken* (1896, 1927, 1946) in some brooding rural novels and a lot of eruptive feminine poetry, both in simple folksong stanzas and in swelling prose rhythms. But the most interesting Modernist poet of the thirties was *Gustaf Munch-Petersen* (1912, 1932, 1938) who died young in Spain, fighting against Franco. He developed rapidly from the Objectivist poetry of *det nøgne menneske* (naked man) (1932) through the Surrealist collections *det underste land* (the land below) (1933) and *mod jerusalem* (toward jerusalem) (1934) to the serenely beautiful *nitten digte* (nineteen poems) (1937). Munch-Petersen was an extremely talented poet (who also wrote poems in Swedish and English published in his collected works) and heralded the new flowering of modern poetry in the forties.

But the thirties were primarily an age of the novel, and most of the novels, the critic Torben Brostrøm has said, were one of two types: Little-Man-What-Now? (the title of Fallada's German bestseller) or A-Child-Was-Hurt (the title of Tove Ditlevsen's childhood novel from 1941) – that is, either dreary social reportage, mostly about white-collar proletarians, or mournful social childhood memoirs in novelistic form.

Jørgen Nielsen (1902, 1929, 1945) wrote incurably, almost masochistically pessimistic novels and short stories about poor Jutland farmers, only slightly relieved by the mordant satire in some of the stories. He is more of a philosophic writer than a social propagandist, and he is primitive in both the good and bad sense of the word. Sometimes his poor Jutland tenants seem to be cousins of the poor whites of the American novel's Deep South; Nielsen has Faulkner's emotions, but not by far Faulkner's language. *Knuth Becker* (1893, 1916, 1974) followed Nexø, also politically, in his excellently written, unfinished and very long series of autobiographical novels beginning with *Det daglige brød* (The Daily Bread) (1932). Becker's giant novel is both social reportage and poetic realism. *Hans Kirk* (1898, 1928, 1962) wanted to write objective novels of historical materialism, and he succeeded in his first book, *Fiskerne* (The Fishermen) (1928), which has rightly become a classic. It is a cool but intense story of the connections between poverty and revivalist Christianity. A third communist novelist, *Hans Scherfig* (1905, 1937, 1979) wrote humorous satires on the bourgeois, on artistic and religious fakes and – in his best book *Det forsømte forår* (The Neglected Spring) (1940) – on the old-fashioned higher education. Scherfig's plots are rather crude and his humorous points a little too obvious, but he is immensely popular and very readable.

Unreadable now, except by social historians, are the proletarian novels of *Harald Herdal* (1900, 1929) and the white-collar dittos of *Leck Fischer* (1904, 1923, 1956). More experimental but hardly more successful are the novels of *Mogens Klitgaard* (1906, 1937, 1945), while *Knud Sønderby* (1909, 1931, 1966) created two minor classics with his first novels, *Midt i en jazztid* (In the Middle of a Jazz Age) and *To mennesker mødes* (Two People Meet) (1932), fragile but nice 'modern love stories', stylistically indebted to Hemingway. Sønderby later excelled in that special Danish genre (usually first printed in newspapers), the informal essay or lyrical causerie, mostly about the weather and the time of the year, as Paludan before and Frank Jæger after him.

An unexpected contribution to the Danish novel came from the Faeroes, from two writers writing in Danish. *Jørgen-Frantz Jacobsen* (1900, 1927, 1938) only wrote one novel, *Barbara* (published posthumously 1939), an intriguing historical romance about an enchanting woman. *William*

71

Heinesen (1900, 1921) published five collections of rather bleak cosmic poetry and two social novels about fishermen before the war, but his fame dates from the post-war period when he wrote two grand collections of poetry – belonging more to the Gaelic world of Dylan Thomas and Hugh Mac Diarmid than to the Danish tradition – and some enchanting, humorous and poetical novels and stories about the strange people inhabiting his stony islands, beginning with *Den sorte gryde* (The Black Pot) (1949) and *De fortabte spillemænd* (The Lost Musicians) (1950). Heinesen reminds one of his great Icelandic neighbour, Halldor Laxness, and if he has not the saga-like power of the Icelandic novelist, he is his equal in humorous and lyrical fabulation.

Contemporary Literature

Older Writers

Isak Dinesen wrote her *Seven Gothic Tales* (1934) in English, and only a year later her own translation was published in Denmark and her real name disclosed: *Karen Blixen* (1885, 1935, 1962). Dinesen was her maiden name, and her father was an author, as were her brother and one of her sisters. The gothic tales were an international success, so was *Out of Africa* (1937), the book about her ten years as a farmer in Kenya. But during the war Karen Blixen turned to her Danish audience – she mostly wrote in Danish from now on, but usually did the English translations herself – with *Vinter-eventyr* (Winter's Tales) (1942) and the pseudonymous gothic entertainment *Gengældelsens veje* (The Angelic Avengers) (1946), a fascinating and weird pastiche. After some shorter books came the two big collections *Sidste fortællinger* (Last Tales) (1957) and *Skæbne-anekdoter* (Anecdotes of Destiny) (1958) and, posthumously, the long story *Ehrengard* (1963) and the heavily edited *Efterladte fortællinger* (Carnival. Entertainments and Posthumous Tales) (1977).

The Africa-book is generally recognized as one of the best books about Africa – but it is more than that. It is a mythical story in its own right about that courage which some people call God. The gothic tales are more difficult to place. They are marvellously entertaining, and Blixen has always had her fervent fans. But the Blixen industry that is growing up both here and in America tends to find level after level of hidden depths in them. It is obvious that Blixen had her 'philosophy', her ideas about love and fate and human beings as marionettes. But it is the working 'philosophy' of a story-teller, not of an existential thinker. She was a story-teller first and last, she always stressed that herself – she was a sister of Sheherezade, she said with characteristic lack of modesty. And she really had something to be proud of. But she has never been placed – as if that is so important! – in Danish literature, although she often showed her indebtedness to classic story-tellers like Blicher and Goldschmidt, and was eagerly accepted by the new generation of the forties as an ally in the fight for imagination. She has not been placed in English or American literature either, and is an outsider like that other bi-lingual mythmaker, Vladimir Nabokov. They have other similarities, too: their liking for the old aristocratic world-order, their artfulness and their brilliant style which does not always conceal a certain 'idling'.

There is no doubt that Karen Blixen is a phenomenon, and a very entertaining and charming one. But one is a little uneasy with her. I am not a great admirer of biographical criticism, and especially not when it comes out with remarks about the dead which would be called gossip if they were said about the living. But I must admit that some of the pieces in the Blixen puzzle suddenly fell into place when I read a few years ago, in one of the many silly and snobbish books about her, that she caught an incurable syphilis in 1913 right after her marriage to a cousin whom she soon after divorced. The theme of tainted virginity really is obsessive in her stories. When one reads, too, that she personally suffered from a fear of touch – she was neurotically afraid of infecting her surroundings – one understands that her distance, her aloofness is not only an aristocratic *noli me tangere* used as a story-teller's device of aesthetic distance, but also a neurosis. This the poet Thorkild Bjørnvig has told in *Pagten* (The Pact) (1974), his wonderful book about his friendship with the Baroness – she did not even need to touch people to influence them. (His anecdote is that she struck the table in Denmark and at the same moment he had a concussion in Paris, and he

Karen Blixen.

believes it). That is the special magic of her stories: they do not really touch you, but they are sure to move you.

Where Karen Blixen was the international lioness, the flamingo, the orchid, the Sheherezade, *Albert Dam* (1880, 1906, 1972) was a Danish pixie, seeming to come right out of one of the hills of Danish popular superstition. His career, or lack of career, must be unique in world literature: two novels when he was 26 and 28, a third when he was 54, and then ten books from his seventieth to his ninetieth year. In the first story he published in a magazine in 1905 – reprinted in his last book, *Tider går* (Times pass – a very significant title) (1970), the whole pattern of his work is already foreshadowed. It is the story of a young son leaving the farm because he can feel that his mother, a widow, needs a new man. The story ends with a description of the night landscape:

> *Den vanddrukne jord lå bugnende hen efter regnens og blæstens ubændige favntag.*

(The water-drenched (literally: water-drunk) earth lay outstretched, bulging after the indomitable embrace of the rain and the wind).

Dam is the mythologist of biological history, and the sentence can be interpreted: the strife between the will of life (the rain, the biological necessity) and the will of man (the wind, free will) results in a making pregnant of the Earth Mother. This idea Dam illustrates – or illuminates – in book after book, novels, stories, essays, a synthesis of Naturalism and Symbolism. Dam's enormous self-taught knowledge from his reading of anthropology and the history of religion, and his enormous self-taught style from reading Nietzsche's Zarathustra and Joyce's Ulysses characterize a work that is both home-grown and universal.

The universe itself was the province of *Jens August Schade* (1903, 1926, 1978) who for more than fifty years poured out books of poetry, novels, plays, all of them bringing the same simple and wonderful dual message: 1) sex is fun, and 2) sex is universal. He is the 'singer of cosmic love on earth'. Schade was neglected or called a pornographer for decades before he was recognized as our most miraculous modern classic. He lived in bohemian poverty, but was never without his red wine and the girls he loved, his 'muses' as he called them. He has much in common with the French surrealists, his belief in the subconscious and in desire is as great as theirs, but he has an earthbound charm totally lacking even in Eluard's sincere poetry of love. He may remind one of an E.E.Cummings without adolescent sentimentality or a Henry Miller without the ego-boasting, but he is a much greater poet.

76

Jens August Schade.

His first book of poetry, *Den levende violin* (The Living Violin – notice the similarity to Chagall) (1926) has the subtitle 'spiritual and sensual songs', and that is the whole point of Schade's work: 'spiritual' and 'sensual' are identical, there is *no* dualism between body and soul. It is impossible *not* to write love poetry. Schade is a universal materialist. It is the same vitalism as in D. H. Lawrence, but socially and psychically untroubled. There is not in Schade as in Lawrence the eternal shifting between theory and fiction and reality. 'Min kvinde er hed / og giver sig hen / som min sang' (my woman is hot / and gives herself / like my song). The word 'like' is all-important, Schade believes in like-ness, which is equality. 'We can never get close enough to each other'. If you can imagine a happy Baudelaire, then you have Schade.

Schade has written a wealth of peotry, as well as novels and plays that are also poetry, totally original erotic dramas and chaotic plot-into-plot-into-plot novels or romances. The best of them, *Mennesker mødes og sød musik opstår i hjertet* (People Meet and Sweet Music Fills the Heart) (1944) came out a few years ago in an American paperback series, but went totally unnoticed, perhaps because the series was too popular. Schade is a poet and neither a philosopher nor a propagandist of licentiousness. But his idyls are full of danger showing that eroticism as transgression which Georges Bataille talks about. The last novel he wrote – he went on publishing beautiful poetry – was called *Jeg er tosset efter dig* (I am Mad About You) (1945) and was about eroticism as a psychosis. It was the closest Schade has been to his great almost-brother-in-name Sade. In that novel one character, with the neat English name Coolglimpse, sings a song in which is the line 'Mit hjerte er en kønsdel' (My heart is a sexual organ). Schade is our greatest heart-musician.

Where both Blixen, Dam and Schade were, so to speak, ready from the start, the other three writers of the pre-war period mentioned here because of their importance in the forties and fifties, were fighters, unsure of their beginnings and unsure when they died, all three prematurely, after lives full of crises.

All the early works of *Paul La Cour* (1902, 1922, 1956) struggle with the problem of belief, belief in beauty, in the outer world, in himself, in political ideas, in the collective consciousness. Only in *Levende vande* (Living Waters) (1946) and *Mellem bark og ved* (Between the Bark and the Wood) (1950) and in the last wonderful poems from Greece, collected in *Efterladte digte* (Posthumous Poems) (1957) did he reach the most natural belief for his vocation, a belief in poetry. For the first twenty-five years La Cour's language and his material were always at odds until he found out that he could make language his material. Or rather the silence that is in language. This materialist mysticism he formulated in his poetics, *Fragmenter af en dagbog* (Fragments of a Diary) (1948), one of the most influential books of the forties and, in my case, one of those unforgettable books of one's youth. The fragments are lyric aphorisms in the style of René Char and Pierre Reverdy, two of La Cour's masters, but simpler than Char and warmer than Reverdy. There is rather too much, when one rereads the book today, of Thou shalt do this and that with thy life, but that is the style – and it comes ultimately from Rilke, who lets his archaic torso of Apollon say: You must change your life. It is a belief in the redeeming force of poetry, not just individually, but collectively, and however much the times they have been a-changing, this force is a fact. Fragmenter af en dagbog is also a document of the Cold War period.

H. C. Branner (1903, 1936, 1966) was a writer who made crises the theme of his novels, and eagerly and sincerely updated his crises with the changing ideological climate. One might also call him a seismograph. His first book, *Legetøj* (Toys) (1936) is a collective novel about a big firm, with a boss who is an obvious Hitler-symbol. Branner's later novels tell private stories about the strong and the weak, culminating in his greatest success, *Rytteren* (The Riding Master) (1949) about a dead riding master and the four people who are still in his power. Branner's anti-hero is the weak humanist with the label-name Clemens, and he becomes a symbol for the 'third standpoint' politics of many intellectuals of the period, torn between East and West in the Cold War. Branner dramatized Rytteren and wrote other plays, which were scenically effective, but rather too after-Ibsen. On the radio, however he triumphed with very experimental plays. It should be noticed at this point that although we have not had really important playwriters since Kjeld Abell, many of our novelists and some of our poets have written plays and even sometimes had them successfully performed. In particular because of a very generous politics of commissions by the State Radio, the radio-play has had a great vogue. Some extremely good literature has come out of this, but unfortunately most of it is not printed, and nobody has ever thought of publishing cheap copies of the performances on tape. In his radio-plays Branner surmounts the lack of balance between psychological 'truth' and symbolic 'meaning' that disturbs his novels. His other undeniable successes are his short stories, especially those about children in *Om lidt er vi borte* (In a Little While We're Gone) (1939) and *To minutters stilhed* (Two Minutes of Silence) (1944) which are so overwhelmingly right that you forget both symbolism and psychology.

Martin A. Hansen (1909, 1935, 1955) started with two social novels in the thirties, during the war he wrote two lively historical novels that were obvious allegories of the resistance movement, in which he took part, and right after the war two experimental collections of short stories, *Tornebusken* (The Thornbush) (1946) and *Agerhønen* (The Partridge) (1947). The novel *Løgneren* (The Liar) (1950), also a radio commission, is his best book, a tight and gripping story about the ethical conflicts between isolated people on a small Danish island. Hansen also published a big unclassifiable book, *Orm og tyr* (Worm and Bull) (1952), a strange mixture of speculation and fact about ancient and medieval Scandinavian beliefs. Hansen was a primary school teacher with a special interest in history, and he was very conscious of his own traditional rural background. In some of his writings there is a tendency to make a cult out of what in Danish is ironically called 'gammelliv' (old-life), homespun rural traditionalism. But the important ethical seriousness of his writing is never in doubt and is very much connected with the Existentialism of the forties in general and, specifically, with the central problem of the resistance movement: the question of moral responsibility when taking part in the liquidation of an informer. The degree of Christian influence (also part of rural and historical traditionalism) on Hansen's ethical fiction has been much debated among critics. At the moment he is rather out of fashion, both because of his subject matter and style – as is H. C. Branner – but his stature is undeniable, and his best short stories and Løgneren, at least, will continue to be read.

New Writers of the Forties

Of the new writers of the forties *Tove Ditlevsen* (1918, 1939, 1976) was the earliest and probably the one most bound to the thirties. She is the most directly confessional writer we have had in Denmark, telling in her poems, short stories and novels all about her working-class childhood, early sexual experiences, marriages and divorces, drug addiction and alcoholism, and psychoses, hospitalizations and suicide attempts. The strange fact is that it is (almost) never embarrassing to read about. She goes through all these experiences with a curious innocence or freshness and a young girl's laughter which is totally disarming. Her language is so obvious, so naked and almost objective even in her most 'sentimental' early poems that she makes one accept sentimentality as a natural human feeling. It is typical of her sardonic humour that she deliberately gave the third volume of her novelistic memoirs the title *Gift* (1971) – as an adjective the Danish word means 'married', but the homonymous noun means 'poison'! Some of her best poems were personal versions of some of Grimm's fairy tales, and in a way everything she wrote was versions of fairy tales, not the H. C. Andersen-type with its double ironies and hidden meanings, but the real, direct, cruel folk tales. Even her last novel, *Vilhelms værelse* (Vilhelm's Room) (1975) about her latest marriage and divorce, with the toughest portraits of living persons in all our literature, reads like a fairy tale, a merry-go-round of princess meets monster and monstress meets prince. Tove Ditlevsen's work is proof that not even psychology can spoil poetry.

Of the other early forties' poets *Piet Hein* (1905, 1940) became famous for his epigrams called *Gruk* (now also in his own English version: Grooks) which belong more to Danish design than to literature. *Halfdan Rasmussen* (1915, 1941) published several collections of serious – very serious – poetry up to 1962, but now only his nonsense poems *Tosserier* (Fooleries) (1951 ff) and his children's rhymes (1949 ff) are read (and sung). His rhymes are terribly funny and lovely. Three attempts at recreating them in English have already been made.

Morten Nielsen (1922, 1943, 1944) is one of the young dead of the Second World War. He died in the resistance movement after publishing just one book, *Krigere uden våben* (Warriors Unarmed) (1943), and he is for Danish poetry what Wilfred Owen – whom he read and admired – was for British poetry of the First World War. His book and the posthumous collection published in 1945 show a great lyrical talent, speaking with authority about a young man's feelings in the shadow of war. Morten Nielsen wrote about love and death with a new beauty and a new desperation.

A more experimental poetry emerged in the early books of *Jørgen Nash* (1920, 1942), *Daggry* (Daybreak) (1942), *Sindets underjord* (Subsoil of the Mind) (1943), *Salvi Dylvo* (1945), and the satirical *Atomelegien* (The Atom Elegy) (1946) – a vital ecstatic surrealism closely connected with the Danish school of young Abstract-Expressionist painters, particularly Asger Jorn, who was Nash's brother. The vitality, naive charm and florid metaphorical language has worn well, and what then seemed wildly avantgarde can now be seen as part of the Danish tradition from Thøger Larsen, Schade and Munch-Petersen. Nash's later development has been away from 'old-fashioned' poetry – he is also a painter – into happenings and other live performances. Another vitalist, *Bundgård Povlsen* (1918, 1944) shows a directly opposite development. From a weak and rather traditional beginning he has slowly developed through a long sequence of works becoming better and better. About 1960 some flowing ode-like poems remind one of Dylan Thomas; Povlsen has the same elementary force. He is still a very uneven poet who flirts a little too much with his own naïveté, but at his best he writes extremely strong, elemental poems.

Ole Sarvig (1921, 1943) is the most important new poet of the forties and to me – and many others – our greatest living writer. As the word 'great' has been used not a few times in this book (I don't think it is a bad word), perhaps I should try to say what I mean by 'great': he has something important and new to say and he says it in a new and perfect way. It is as simple as that.

Sarvig is a poet, a novelist, a playwright, an essayist and an art critic. Poetry came first and is still his greatest achievement: the cycle of five books from 1943 to 1948 (in later selections and in an excellent German translation given the collective title *Den sene dag* (Late Day)), consisting of *Grønne digte* (Green Poems), the prose poem *Mangfoldighed* (Multitude), *Jeghuset* (The I-House), the prose poem *Legende* (Legend) and *Menneske* (Man). To this cycle is added *Min kærlighed* (My Love) (1952), consisting of three poems and an experimental 'drama for an open door', some other, smaller books and, in 1974, the large collection *Forstadsdigte* (Suburban Poems).

Then comes the cycle of novels: *Stenrosen* (The Stone Rose) (1955), *De sovende* (The Sleepers) (1958), *Havet under mit vindue* (The Sea Under My Window) (1960), *Limbo* (1963) and *Glem ikke* (Do Not Forget) (1972). His dramatic experiments continued in *Stemmer i Mørket* (Voices In the Dark) (1970), an 'oratorio' and a radio-play, the play *Sejlads* (Sea Voyage) (1974) and *I lampen* (In the Lamp) (also 1974) which is called a 'skærmnovelle', a short story for television.

In between are the essays, philosophical reportage from Europe, *Midtvejs i det tyvende århundrede* (Midway in the

Twentieth Century) (1950); personal comments on New Testament texts in *Evangeliernes billeder* (Images of the Gospels) (1953); collections of miscellaneous essays *Glimt* (Glimpses) (1956) and *I går – om lidt* (Yesterday – In a Moment) (1976). And Sarvig's art criticism – he is our only important modern art critic – in *Edvard Munchs grafik* (E. M.'s Graphic Art) (1948), *Krisens billedbog* (Picture-Book of the Crisis) (1950) and *Stedet, som ikke er* (The Non-Existent Place) (1966). And other books . . ..

A great number of the essays are self-commentary, where Sarvig tries to formulate, in intellectual terms, the vision of life and human existence and of art that is expressed as art in the two cycles of poetry and novels. The essays have been mostly resisted by the critics, even those who admire the fictional works. But they are a necessary part of the Sarvig corpus, not because they 'explicate' what is 'implicit' in the poems and novels – they can speak for themselves – but for their own artistic value in the holistic system which is Sarvig's world. The tone of voice in the essays can become somewhat sacerdotal, I admit, but their intention is not to convert the reader but to illuminate the world. Sarvig's 'metaphysics' can actually quite easily be apprehended as what it primarily is: a frame of reference for an artistic vision. But Sarvig's non-confessional religious ideas and emotions are, of course, not there just to 'give you metaphors for your poetry' (as the spirits said to Yeats). They are part of a coherent historical view, not unconnected with Spengler's pessimistic cultural philosophy about 'the destruction of the occident' (Untergang des Abendlandes), to which Sarvig's title 'The Late Day' obviously refers. In his view of art, too, the development is a fall from the innocence of impressionism to the darkly symbolic abstract painting.

The five books of Sarvig's poetic cycle express this development as a symbolic drama in five acts: Innocence of the world (Green Poems), Immense variety of the world (Multitude),

Ole Sarvig.

The constitution of the self (The I-House), The dream of love and death (Legend) and The new composite being of I-and-Thou in actual love (Man).

I think it could be argued that the five novels are a retrograde movement through the same phases: The Stone Rose, an intense, almost surrealistic reportage from the ruins of Berlin is the last act in negative – The Sleepers, a crime story with a Graham Greene-surface is the dream of love and death in negative – The Sea Under My Window, another 'adventure story', is the loss of Ego as the negative of the constitution of the Self – Limbo is the shimmering, buzzing summer land of pre-war premonitions – and Do Not Forget is an ironic satirical play of transformed innocence.

In the poetry: the Creation – the Multitude – the I – the

Dream – the You. In the novels: The You (in the plural) – The Dream – the I-less – the Multitude – the Re-Creation.

I do not wish to set up Sarvig as an 'original thinker', but I would like to indicate the interchangeability of aesthetics and ethics (and religion) in his 'system'.

It all exists for the vision, in the double sense of sight and in-sight (the double dream of spring, to quote John Ashbery's title). There is in Sarvig's poems, and in the novels, too, especially in Limbo, a marvellous visionary power which makes him write as a painter paints. The new-ness of his work is also a painter's – almost an a-literary novelty. To see the world as new. In an old and decaying civilization certainly. Almost at the bottom of the fall. True. But still with eyes to see and hands to touch. Exuberance is beauty, said Blake. I think Sarvig's greatness is his exuberance.

In 1978, Sarvig published a new novel, *De rejsende* (The Travellers) which must be the first of a trilogy, as it follows very closely in structure the first part of Dante's Divine Comedy. Sarvig's hero with the very obvious name Dan T. Larsen travels through Europe at the end of the present century. The book begins with some beautifully evocative chapters in Moscow and Leningrad, described in such loving detail that you would think Sarvig had lived there all his life. The shadow that follows Sarvig's hero is his long dead communist father. The Travellers is a political allegory about twentieth century history and far beyond. Here too Sarvig uses elements from popular literature and film, spy-plots and underground activities. His visionary novel works on many levels; it is extremely packed but never obscure. It is Sarvig's message about 'European man', living by grace and under judgment, and the judgment is his consciousness, the constraint and despair of social and psychological ideologies. Against this Sarvig sets the sensuous richness of the world, Grace.

Thorkild Bjørnvig (1918, 1947) is a lyrical poet in the old, grand style, signified by the names of the poets he has recre-

Thorkild Bjørnvig.

ated in translation: Hölderlin, Baudelaire, Rilke. Bjørnvig was recognized as a master from the start, with *Stjærnen bag gavlen* (The Star Behind the Gable) (1947), his first book of intense and lovely philosophical love poetry. In *Anubis* (1955), *Figur og ild* (Figure and Fire) (1959) and *Vibrationer* (1966) he continued to chisel out majestic stanzas of great impact, culminating in the long poem *Ravnen* (The Raven) (1968), which rightly deserves the Danish description 'tanketung', which means 'thought-heavy' (thought-laden) – to me it is impenetrable. Recently, Bjørnvig has made a new beginning with *Delfinen* (The Dolphin) (1975), fighting for a good cause against pollution, but still with the old, heavy pathos, and especially with *Pagten* (The Pact) (1974), a book about his dangerous friendship with Karen Blixen, ostensibly a memoir, but reading more like a novel, and a very good one, too, showing more of Bjørnvig's Olympic humour than has been revealed in his poetry, and also showing to best advantage his penetrating gifts as a critic. I do not want to seem ungrateful, for Bjørnvig's best poems are enormously impressive and moving, but I do think his poetry is an example of a stylization expressing a psychic regression – and that it very often sounds more like Swinburne and early Lowell than like Rilke.

If Bjørnvig is too heavy, *Frank Jæger* (1926, 1948, 1977) is too easy. Or rather, he suffered from the popularity of the easy side of his great literary talent, his Danish charm and youthful irresponsibility. One of his most bitter poems is the title poem of *Cinna* (1959) where the 'wrong' Cinna, the poet, is killed by the mob while insisting that 'jeg er ikke den I tror' (I am not the one you think) – this is the *second* Frank Jæger-myth. The first myth is the charming young loafer, eternally in love, who is the main character of Jæger's first three volumes of poetry, beginning with *Dydige digte* (Virtuous Poems) (1948), and his first three prose works, ending with *Den unge Jægers lidelser* (Suffering of the young Hunter – the name Jæger means hunter) (1953), his perfectly charming and lying pseudo-memoirs at the age of 27. The second myth is the suffering vacuum, the unproductive (with a score of books!) echo chamber for Classic and Romantic writers, with Sophus Claussen as the main burden of the poetry and Karen Blixen as the featherweight weighing down the many self-consciously tradition-haunted short stories. Frank Jæger's masks are fascinating as well as a little scaring and demoniac by their indication that behind the last fake emptiness there is a real emptiness and even this might not be a sickness to death but 'just' an allergy. But when all is said the perfection of the lyric poet Frank Jæger is still there, an untranslatable poet with an absolute ear for the tiniest nuances of the Danish language. Several lines from his poems come to mind, expressing a magic music of metrical rhythm and phonetic pattern. One line goes like this: *Esbønderup, det hvide hospital* which is just a place name in North Zealand, with the words 'the white hospital' added, but it is a rhythmical and phonetic harmony which has haunted me for twenty years or more. Frank Jæger was a magician of language.

In 1945 came the first books of two poets who in the seventies have both become enormously influential political poets, *Erik Knudsen* (1922, 1945) and *Ivan Malinovski* (1926, 1945). Knudsen had his earliest great success with his third book, *Blomsten og sværdet* (The Flower and the Sword) (1949), a collection of poems showing a typical fortyish split between religious-poetical doubt and political commitment, but in a Modernist metaphorical and rhythmical language which made a great impression. 'These poems will be learned by heart,' the always perceptive Tom Kristensen wrote in his review, and he was right; I for one can still recite most of the poems in Blomsten og sværdet. In Knudsen's later books from the fifties there are also extremely good poems, but they are more and more filled with an unproductive opposition between 'being a poet' and 'being in the world', so that when Knudsen chooses the latter opportunity in his Brechtian plays and pamphlet poetry in the sixties and seventies it feels almost like a happy release. Both Knudsen and Malinovski were heavily indebted to the great renewers of Swedish poetry in the forties – Ekelöf, Lindegren, Vennberg –, Malinovski so much so that he has discarded his first books and wants *Galgenfrist* (Short Respite) (1958) recognized as his début. Malinovski is our best translator of poetry from several languages. His recreation of Pasternak, for example, is the only one in any Western language (as far as I know) which makes one understand that Pasternak is a major poet. His own poetry, too, is strongly influenced by Modernist poetry in general more than by any specific masters (although Brecht is oppressively present in the later books), and his language does come dangerously close to an international 'modernese'. The poems make you suspicious because they translate too easily. However, they are often strikingly beautiful, with metaphorical patterns which make a New Critic's mouth water. His development from aristocratic nihilism to populist Communism is typical of the change of ideological climate from the forties to the seventies, but it is sincere and not opportunist.

The war experience which conditioned the first commitment of Knudsen's and Malinovski's poetry has also been the deciding influence on two very good but almost provocatively traditionalist novelists, *Erik Aalbæk Jensen* (1928, 1949) and *Tage Skou-Hansen* (1925, 1957). Skou-Hansen's first book, *De nøgne træer* (The Naked Trees) (1957) was an essay in moral psychology about the resistance movement, and his latest novel, *Den hårde frugt* (Hard Fruit) (1977) confronts the main characters from then with their sons and daughters, the political activists of the seventies. After five more or less successful novels in the old style Aalbæk Jensen has started on an impressive series of novels about the experiences of his generation before, during and after the war. – *Perleporten* (The Pearly Gate) (1964) is the first, a wonderfully clear and compassionate description of a Jutland parish. *Sagen* (The Case) (1971) takes us up to the present with an absorbing story about an affair of local development, and *Kridtstregen* (The Chalk Line) (1976) goes back to the occupation, describing two Danish deserters from the German Army on the run through the country, hunted by both the Germans and the Danish resistance movement. Aalbæk Jensen paints a panoramic picture of Danish history from the thirties to the seventies, and the books are so good that one forgets their anachronistic form.

Elsa Gress (1919, 1945) belongs to the forties, but has provided an important ferment in Danish literature in the following decades. She is a novelist, playwright, filmmaker, an excellent memoir-writer, and one of our leading translators of modern American literature but most of all, she is the salt – often very coarse-grained – in the cultural debate in Denmark. She gives her opinions (and their priority) in an interminable stream of essays, always very well-informed, especially about American literature and politics, and often not only righteous but also right. She can be extremely irritating, but her intelligence and indefatigability are truly impressive. Another cultural hero of the forties is *Thorkild Hansen* (1927, 1947), a very unusual travel writer and historical biographer, whose well-documented books are more philosophical fiction than history. His books about Danish expeditions to Arabia and Greenland and about the Danish eighteenth-century colonies in Africa – all translated into English – and his latest success, a documentary about the process against Knut Hamsun in Norway in 1945, are absorbing to read, but leave, at least with me, an ambiguous taste in the mouth because of the implied hero-worship and fatalism, in the wake of Hansen's great inspiration, André Malraux.

New Writers of the Fifties

About 1950 a group of lyric poets emerged, of whom *Jørgen Gustava Brandt* (1929, 1949) and *Per Højholt* (1928, 1949) are the two most interesting. Brandt had his single but enormous theme ready from the start: epiphany, the Zen-like illumination of the moment. With *Fragment af imorgen* (Fragment of Tomorrow) (1960) he found a form for it, a loose but very rhythmical free verse development which reminds one of jazz improvisation. In many books in the sixties and seventies Brandt developed this theme, often a little too self-consciously for one denying the importance of being an ego. Many of his poems are about the centre of Copenhagen where he grew up, effectively using the symbolic implications of the Danish name for this part of town, 'den indre by' (the inner city). Brandt is a non-religious mystic whose lines often borrow the beauty of the world. Højholt is a daringly experimental poet whose results are perhaps less interesting than his methods, which he has explained – if you can call it that – in his essays on poetics *Cézannes metode* (C.'s Method) (1967) and *Intethedens grimasser* (The Grimaces of Nothingness) (1972). Højholt is a tireless inventor of linguistic gimmicks, and he has had a great and healthy influence on many younger writers.

Jørgen Sonne (1925, 1950) is also a sort of innovator, with the grand purpose of renewing poetical diction in Denmark. His critical master is Ezra Pound, and he tirelessly translates European poetry from the Renaissance to Modernism into his own language, his very own rather quirky language, which in his original poems stretches and compresses rhythm and metaphors in often fascinating ways. *Robert Corydon* (1924, 1950) is in a long series of rather dull books a painter of the world as metaphor. In *Uffe Harder*'s poetry (1930, 1954) French and Spanish surrealism fight with an original, nervously intense talent. *Erik Stinus* (1934, 1958) is another internationalist, a Third World specialist, whose metaphorical tapestries can seem a little impersonal, although the human commitment is impressive. *Cecil Bødker* (1927, 1955) has written charming poetry of feminine sensibility as well as both traditional and experimental prose, but has achieved most – including international fame – as one of our best writers of children's fiction.

From 1948 to 1953 the literary magazine *Heretica* was the platform of the new generation of writers, 'the writers of the forties' – with Bjørnvig, Martin A. Hansen, Frank Jæger and Tage Skou-Hansen among its distinguished editors. Heretica's continuation *Vindrosen* (The Wind Rose) was taken over by the next generation and from 1959 to 1964 was edited by Klaus Rifbjerg and Villy Sørensen, two leading new writers, who made it into an extraordinarily lively magazine which included all the best poets and prose-writers and critics. Especially important were the polemical contributions of the critic *Torben Brostrøm* (1927, 1960), who as a latter-day Brandes attacked the backwardness of Danish literature – forty years as usual – and promoted the new poets very effectively under the brandname of 'Modernism'. This was not totally wrong. There certainly was a new awareness of European Modernism and many good translations were made. The movement also led to the revaluation of earlier Danish modernists such as Sophus Claussen (who had already been important to the Heretica-people but who was now reinterpreted by Brostrøm in Jungian terms and by New Criticism methods) and Gustaf Munch-Petersen. Nevertheless the picture was a little more complicated. An opposition between the '1948-Heretica-generation' and '1960-Modernism' was too polemical to be the whole truth. Perhaps a philosophical parallel can indicate the differences: the literature of the forties was written by existentialists, and the new writers at the end of the fifties were phenomenologists. This is obvious in the case of new prose writers such as Villy Sørensen (who had been a student of Heidegger's in Freiburg), Poul Vad and Peter Seeberg (who was also greatly influenced by Wittgenstein). And the new 'physiological' poetry which Brostrøm found in his poets and which was certainly characteristic of Klaus Rifbjerg had an obvious parallel in Merleau-Ponty's ideas about 'the world as body'. (In the same way many phenomena in the later sixties are parallel with French structuralism. In the whole period there was certainly a great interest in the changing fashions of French philosophy, but I am not interested in direct influences, I just wish to indicate that parallels between the literature of the three decades and the existentialist, phenomenological and structuralist movements are important.)

Klaus Rifbjerg (1931, 1956) is a very good poet, and I must emphasize from the start that I dissent from most of my colleagues among Danish critics in my evaluation of his work. I shall explain why. In the general consciousness, and for many people who would never think of reading him, he is *the* modern writer in Denmark, and he himself has not exactly tried to diminish this image. This is not to say that Rifbjerg is a media phenomenon, although he is that, too, but he is more than that. He is a typical example of a totality which is greater than the sum of its parts. And what a lot of parts! Rifbjerg has from 1956 till now published more than fifty books. I would not say that he is too prolific, either, it does come natural to him (most of it). But I am afraid that he is a repetition of the phenomenon noted in the cases of Oehlenschläger and Johannes V. Jensen: the enormously talented young writer, who breaks through with a few sensationally new and good books, and then goes on and on and on. My dilemma is the critic's, who is extremely happy when a good book comes out and who has learnt to accept the law of nature that most books are bad. What is absolutely unbearable is the disappointment when a good writer is not good *enough!* The standard new Rifbjerg book three or four times a year is usually not good enough, but contains glimpses of his fantastic talent, which occasioned a renewal of Danish literary language with his fourth and fifth book, *Konfrontation* (1960) and *Camouflage* (1961).

I think I can indicate what the trouble is. It is certainly not dishonesty. He is a singularly straightforward and agreeable person (except of course when criticizing critics, that's only natural). Neither is it lack of ability. He has genius. The problem is psychology. Rifbjerg is an ego-poet, with memory as his material, and he has once and for all, in those two books of poetry, undertaken the literary equivalent of a psychoanalysis. (And like many people who have been through an ordinary analysis he has become loquacious and has a problem with his ego-identification – we all seem to be him). Left to him is only a broken heap of images, the ruins of

Klaus Rifbjerg.

memories of his personal life, which he tries to vivify with his enormous linguistic gifts and to update with parallels to the changing cultural and political situation. If his 'physiological' poetry, his 'confrontation'-poetry, as the type has been called after his book, illustrates the axioms about 'the world as body' and 'the world as language', he seems to have canalized these dicta into a simpler formulation: 'the body as I'.

In his novels, especially – for Rifbjerg still writes good poems occasionally, though his plays are negligible – the dilemma is obvious. His identification with his fictional characters is psychologically and aesthetically unsound. It is fluctuating. He goes in and out of them in an almost indecent way, lets them speak (the novels are often in the first person) with both his very distinctive and 'their own' voices, and he comments on them, directly and indirectly, favourably and unfavourably. The plots are the usual plots of entertainment novels – with autobiographical colouring – but the 'moral psychology' and the 'commitment to currently debated topics' and especially in some passages the language, make the books pretend to more.

The new thing that happened in a new language in 1960 in Konfrontation was exactly what the title says: a spontaneous confrontation between a young, intelligent and sensitive man and the modern world, an almost aggressive leave–taking of the old poetical language and embracing of the technical vocabulary of science, as in the programmatic poem 'Terminology':

Ja, ja, ja nu kommer jeg	Yes, yes, yes now I come
ned til jer	down to you
ord.	words.
Trompet: forblæst.	Trumpet: blown out.
Skov: vissen.	Wood: faded.
Karyatide: antik.	Caryatid: antique.
Kærlighed: løgn.	Love: lie.
Halleluja: ræb.	Hallelujah: belch.
Poesi: hvor er mit brokbind?	Poetry: where is my hernial truss?

Opvågnen fra nedfrosset	Awakening from frozen
dybtanæsticeret koma	deeply anestheticized coma
rykvis.	spasmodically.
Udflod: smag.	Discharge: taste.
Transfocator: syn.	Transfocator: vision.
Valens: værdi.	Valence: worth.
Pessar: virkelighed.	Diaphragm: reality.
Mach: romantik.	Mach: romance.
Lyrik: 5-4-3-2-1-0.	Lyric: 5-4-3-2-1-0.

The count down to zero (cf. Gelsted's young student blowing up the show boat, who is rejected in the next poem in Rifbjerg's book) continues in extremely energetic and exciting poems, some of the best being about Rifbjerg's experience of the United States. And the leading up to the explosion, not of the word but of the ego, continues in Camouflage the following year. This is a long experimental poem about a journey into the interior (the womb) to find 'the new sensibility', a recreation of the nine months of creation, ending with the cry of the newborn, not with a bang but a whimper. There are some avantgarde mannerisms, but it is a great and very moving poem.

However, Rifbjerg's umbilical cord was not cut after all but stretched out into fifty books of poetry, fiction and drama, with more to come. In almost all of these books his wonderful talent makes guest appearances. One of his latest novels, *Et bortvendt ansigt* (An Averted Face) (1977), is a trivial story about A married to B and with C as his lover getting saved from suicide by D, the natural young girl of the people (the one who found the golden horns), and has all the current topics such as women's liberation, middle-aged men's death-urge and 'love in our time' mixed in for 'a good read'. And then suddenly we have a prose poem about cigarettes (on page 24 and continued on page 27) a Francis Ponge-like description of existence:

> The cigarettes are lying on the table next to the bed, and I sling my legs out and sit up to take them. The smell of sulphur from the match makes the little hairs on the neck bristle, and when the smoke from the cigarette reaches the critical point in the passage from mouth to throat the whole body contracts in protest. The nicotine and the other substances which I don't know make the little capillaries everywhere astringent, I get dizzy and feel cold, I want to put out the cigarette but go on smok-

ing, I start to tell myself again about being sensible, but, little by little, as the poisonous substances in the tobacco meet those already deposited in the body by thousands upon thousands of other cigarettes a sort of physiological armistice sets in, a form of anaesthesia with irritability and horror pushed down so far under certain protective strata that the world begins to look ordinary. I get up with the cigarette in my mouth and go to the window to pull the curtain. ... I put out the cigarette and light a new one. ... I have started tasting the cigarette, it doesn't hurt anywhere now. I try to find out what the taste is like, but that is not possible. Once, many years ago, cigarettes had a taste of something, something special, and I know it was tobacco. Now they only taste of burnt cotton, but that is better than that icy feeling of vascular cramp which the first, unprepared-for one always brings about. I am getting normal.

Villy Sørensen (1929, 1953) is a short story writer and essayist of great ability. Where Rifbjerg is (or was) the provocateur, Sørensen is the sage. When he speaks everyone in Denmark listens, even the politicians. His three collections of short stories and four books of essays are among the most important books stylistically, too, published in Denmark in the last twenty-five years, with their mellow, ironical, often paradoxical thought-language, inspired by Kierkegaard, but also by Thomas Mann, Hermann Broch and, especially, Robert Musil. He has also written a book about Kafka's work, introductions to Schopenhauer and Nietzsche, and recently a monograph on *Seneca* (1976), in which Sørensen is actually more interesting than Seneca. The list of names indicates his placing, among the poet-thinkers, as a non-academic (but soundly academically based) philosopher, with ethics, and more and more that special branch of ethics called politics, as his province.

Villy Sørensen.

His first two books, a selection of which was published in English, *Sære historier* (Strange Stories) (1953) and *Ufarlige historier* (Harmless Stories) (1955), are absurd and grotesque fairy tales, legends and short stories, told with charmingly innocent irony, stories about philosophical problems disguised as moral conflicts disguised as nihilism. His third book of stories, *Formynderfortællinger* (Guardian Tales) (1964) is more 'serious', but just as elegant and just as explosive in its hidden philosophical depths. That almost all of Sørensen's less than thirty stories allude to other literature and are often direct versions or perversions of other stories (medieval legends, H. C. Andersen, and others) could be seen as a sort of fictional sterility, but is more fairly interpreted as proof of a deep commitment to European culture from ancient Greece and Rome to Kafka and Heidegger.

Sørensen is the type of writer who does not act, but reacts, and his reactions are extremely intelligent and provocative. Consequently the difference between his stories and his essays is rather insignificant – just the 'fiction', and perhaps even his 'utopianism' is a sort of 'fiction'. But in both genres his deep irony and his wisdom excel. The first book of essays, *Digtere og dæmoner* (Poets and Demons) (1959), was mostly about literature, the second, *Hverken – eller* (Neither – Nor, with a typical pun on Kierkegaard's title) (1961) and the third, *Mellem fortid og fremtid* (Between the Past and the Future, with an equally typical significant circumscription of 'just now') (1969) were more miscellaneous and topical, with comments on both literature and philosophy and social, pedagogical and political matters. Still, the unity is obvious, not just the unity of Sørensen's clever mind, but also of his strict and compassionate vision. Sørensen speaks in 1969 about 'the frustrating gap between what is theoretically possible and what is practically impossible', and this is the gap he tries to fill with his latest and most ambitious book of essays, *Uden mål – og med* (Purposeless and Purposeful – but with an untranslatable pun in the Danish title) (1973). Sørensen's maieutic method here seems to me to be troubled by uncertainty about the identity of the imaginary reader, who is that centaurian monster, the philosopher-politician. However, the book is brilliant, thought-provoking, and maybe action-provoking, too. In 1978 Sørensen published *Oprør fra midten* (Revolt from the Centre), a widely discussed political pamphlet written in cooperation with a professor of technology and an a-typical humanitarian politician. The book amounts to a political programme, with Sørensen running the risk of getting into bad company with his alternatives to the often excessively square Marxism that has dominated the Danish cultural milieu in recent years. But it is an honest attempt to put the theories of the philosopher-poet into practice, not without parallels with the so-called 'new philosophers' in France. It remains to be seen if Sørensen, by heroically interfering with the practical policy of the welfare state, has moved closer to or further away from his own centre as a writer. What is certain is that 'Oprør fra midten' has occasioned the most meaningful public debate in Denmark for many years, and the rings from the philosopher's stone he threw are beginning to spread (through translations) to other countries.

Peter Seeberg (1925, 1956) is also, in a way, a philosophical writer, but only in fiction – four novels and three collections of short stories till now. He is an innovative and very successful director of a provincial museum, and says that he only publishes a book when he has something to say – thereby implying that certain other Danish writers perhaps publish too much. This is typical of the dogged moral strictness of Seeberg, which is very often relieved, however, by an Olympian smile. Seeberg's first novel, *Bipersonerne* (The Secondary Characters) (1956), is a terse story about compulsorily levied foreign workers in Berlin 1943, a realistic myth about human lack of contact, about the psychic tropisms of random existence, written in a phenomenologically tense, 'objective' prose style. *Fugls føde* (Bird's Scrapings) (1957) also, is a philosophical fable about the dire necessities of life, symbolized in a Wittgensteinian proposition which is formulated as a demand by the main character's friend – or 'guru' or 'anima' –: 'Write something that is real'. Seeberg dramatizes the 'realistic' writer's dilemma, but he does more than that. The conclusion is both an aesthetics and an ethics: 'Reality is not unimportant, Tom, everybody must find his starting-point in despair and then proceed as best he can'. The central character is called Tom – a symbolical name, being the hononym in Danish of the adjective 'tom', which means 'empty'. Seeberg's third book, *Eftersøgningen* (The Search) (1962), seventeen very short stories, is a little too abstract in the absurdist manner, with characters with Beckett-names, but it contains masterpieces like 'The Spy', an intensely moving realistic fable about being a spy in the house of reality. *Hyrder* (Shepherds) (1970) is a very different book, a very intense, almost nervously blurred novel about people who are both helpless and each other's helpers. One is reminded of T. S. Eliot's plays, but Hyrder is much better fiction. Seeberg's philosophical myth about Being in the World is written with almost evangelical purity. Recently, he has published two almost bewilderingly rich collections of short prose, *Dinosaurens sene eftermiddag* (The Late Afternoon of the Dinosaur) (1974) and *Argumenter for benådning* (Arguments for a Reprieve) (1976), a patterned wilderness of fables, myths and pastiches of folklore and documentary material (inspired by his museum work) and seemingly 100 per cent realistic short stories – reminding me of Katherine Anne Porter – and terrible Borges-like tales such as 'Wingbeats' about an eight-year-old boy who decides not to live because life is not perfect. The two books are a virtuoso performance, certainly, but they are also a hymn to life's multiplicity and magnitude. In a way they seem to be Seeberg's answer to the recent insistent and rather silly demand for a popular and documentary art: he creates a story-world that has both the power of anonymous folk art and the humility of the great poet.

Ved havet (At the Seaside) (1978) is Seeberg's lightest and most friendly novel, brilliantly concretizing essential philosophical problems. Are we free when we enjoy our 'free time'? – is the basic theme of this series of variations about a summer Sunday on a Danish island, 'a day that embraces every lack of continuity'. The wonderful precision of Seeberg's observations expresses a deep solidarity with the common life that makes Ved havet more of a political novel than all the obvious sermons by amateur writers recently published.

Poul Vad (1927, 1956) is certainly a 'documentary' novelist in a series of novels written after a rather derivative first book of poetry: *De nøjsomme* (Modest People) (1960), *Taber og vinder* (Loser and Winner) (1967) and *Dagen før livet begynder* (The Day Before Life Begins) (1970) – but he is much more than that. I suspect that Poul Vad – who is also a very good art critic – wants to *paint* the phenomenology of modernity in the guise of 'realistic' and 'semi-autobiographical' novels, paint it in different colours from book to book, as the covers indicate, grey in the first book – ostensibly an 'objective' report about young middle-class intellectual couples in the fifties, content with little and afraid of demanding anything serious from life – white and black in the second book, influenced by 'nouveau roman' and French film, in the anonymous narrator's slow, careful description of the impenetrability of the world, alienation as 'écriture' – and blue and green in the third volume, a very funny and desperate stream-of-consciousness about some of the characters from the first book in an earlier period of life, in a camp for conscientious objectors. Vad does not make it easy for his readers, but he rewards their patience with a coherent fictional universe in which it is good to be. His next book was very different, almost a satirical play as an epilogue to the three great non-tragedies. *Rubruk* (1972) uses a medieval Dutch monk's report about his travels in Asia (translated into Danish a few years before in a collection of historical sources) to build an indigenous fable about belief and bewilderment as equally necessary factors for human existence. On one level Vad competes with Mann's and Hesse's oriental fables, but the book is also a sceptical and ironical comment on the ideological debate of the seventies. Its wisdom and gaiety are beautiful. Its colour is deep blue.

Poul Vad's latest novel, *Kattens anatomi* (The Anatomy of the Cat) (1978) is a gigantic story of six hundred pages about a short train trip in 1936, involving a whole tapestry of built-in episodes from all over the world and many periods, beginning with creation. The book is a technical feat, obviously written in conscious competition with other international novelists of the seventies, e. g. Thomas Pynchon. The new Latin-American novel, in particular, must have been a great influence and a challenge: why can't it happen here, in Denmark? The rightly famous 'boom' in Latin-American literature must be a similar challenge to many other small nations, and Poul Vad is, as far as I know, one of the first writers to take it up. The important thing, of course, is that 'Kattens anatomi' is a very good novel. Its international pretensions are interesting – and justified.

Among the other new novelists of the fifties, *Leif Panduro* (1923, 1957, 1977), Rifbjerg's friend and competitor, is the most important. He became immensely popular for his novels and especially for his television plays which kept most of the population at home to watch the moral entanglements of persons like themselves, though generally a little higher in the social hierarchy. Panduro's plays were immensely effective and first-class entertainment, as are his novels, which lack not only the literary pretensions of Rifbjerg but also his genius. Panduro seems to have taken most of his ideas for plots from other current fiction – Max Frisch, John Updike and the like, but he twists and turns them with a very neurotic Danish humour. (Danes themselves always mention the famous Danish sense of humour). His first success, *Rend mig i traditionerne* (Kick me in the Traditions) (1958) is very close to Salinger's Catcher in the Rye, and has become just as beloved in Denmark by succeeding generations of young people. In *Øgledage* (Lizard Days) (1961) he showed that he could be just as 'modernistic' as the other new writers, but generally his novels are straight 'good stories', very often about a man going mad and thereby proving his sanity and the madness of the world. Panduro's art strikes an uneasy balance between wish-fulfilment and real art, but is always immensely entertaining.

More pretentious and more flawed are the novels and stories of *Peter Ronild* (1928, 1959) who plays up a romantic tough-guy temperament against realistic description in a colourful style with many 'original' metaphors. The novel *Kroppene* (The Bodies) (1964) is his best and technically most accomplished. After the Rifbjerg-generation a group of 'new realists' was launched, but later dropped by the younger critics as too 'bourgeois'. *Anders Bodelsen* (1937, 1959) was a conscientious suburbanist, but has changed to suspense stories – with international success – in the wake of Simenon and Patricia Highsmith, no great loss to literature but a good gain for crime readers. *Christian Kampmann* (1939, 1962) has been hailed as a 'new Herman Bang' for his short stories and novels of bourgeois sensibility, gently satirized, but whereas Bang was an avantgarde inventor, Kampmann is eau de Cologne.

New Writers of the Sixties

Of the new poets writing about 1960 *Benny Andersen* (1929, 1960) has become extremely popular, and rightly so, for his chaplinesque charades of puns and striking imagery, creating a sad and humorous character, the 'little man' of today. The metaphorical inventiveness and endearing human qualities of the poems are extraordinary, although a certain repetitiveness cannot be helped – Andersen himself seems to be a little tired of his character. However with *Svantes viser* (Svante's Songs) (1972) he had a renewed and seemingly everlasting success. It is a series of sad and funny songs with Andersen's own tunes (he began his career as a bar pianist) and with a connecting prose commentary. The songs have been recorded and are on the hit lists etcetera, 'but' they are still good poetry – and have already added several quotations to popular wisdom, like 'life is not the worst thing we have'. This knowledge characterizes all of Benny Andersen's intensely human and lovely poems.

The most *un*-popular poet of his generation is *Jess Ørnsbo* (1932, 1960), and that is understandable. He is a wild nihilist whose interpretation of 'the world as body' seems to be 'the world as intestines'. The speaker in his poems appears to be an inhabitant of a dustbin left over from Beckett's Endgame, but I must admit that Ørnsbo's poetry of faeces and vomit – though often a too easy transfer of personal neuroses into a universal slum area – sometimes reaches apocalyptic heights.

Poul Borum (1934, 1962) has published an annual collection of poems since *Livslinier* (Life Lines) (1962) and also functioned as a critic, with among other works *Poetisk modernisme* (1966), an introduction to European and American poetry since Baudelaire and Whitman. He trusts that his position in Danish literature will be secure enough without further mention in this book.

Inger Christensen (1935, 1962) is the most important member of the sixties-generation. Her first two books of poetry, *Lys* (Light) (1962) and *Græs* (1963) certainly belong to the new 'physiological' poetry, but with an intensity of feminine sensibility, which makes them stand apart. Rimbaud is the main character of 'Meeting', the long hymnic poem in the second book, and Christensen has much of Rimbaud's desperation and power in her own wild language. The novel *Evighedsmaskinen* (Perpetuum Mobile) (1964) is a retelling of the Resurrection with a brilliant satirical first part and many deep insights, but it becomes diluted into lyricism. Her second novel *Azorno* (1967) is a great success, however, and has been the subject of many sophisticated interpretations because of its intricate formal pattern. Azorno is a sort of Chinese box-novel with a series of narrators, each renouncing the former. But it is also a fable of love and jealousy, with womens' liberation symbolized by the maenads tearing Orpheus asunder. It is an infinitely enjoyable and very

Inger
Christensen.

difficult book. Inger Christensen's next book *Det* (It, or That,
or The) (1969) is even more intricately patterned, but easily
readable. It was both an enormous critical success – the book
of the decade! – and a bestseller. It was – and still is – quoted
in politicians' speeches, on squatters' posters, in advertise-
ments for progressive architecture, and set to music by both
rock groups and 'serious' composers. *Det* is a difficult book to
describe. It is both a collection of poems and one long poem,
organized in a lattice of parameters, of which the two most
prominent are a creation myth – mirrored in the three parts
of the book, called Pro-Logos, Logos and Epi-Logos – and the
splitting up of the middle part, Logos, into three chapters,
The Scene, The Action and The Text, each consisting of eight
series of eight poems each, cross-related. The series are

named after the categories in the great Danish linguist Viggo Brøndal's book about the theory of prepositions, and they are actually pre-positions for an interpretation of the world. (The eight categories are: symmetries, transitivities, continuities, connexities, variabilities, extensions, integrities and universalities). This short resumé, of course, cannot show what riches the strict systems of the book contain. It is even more difficult to say what it is about. In a way *Det* is a *summa* of the philosophical and ideological debate of the sixties, with many references to French structuralism and British anti-psychiatry. But Blake, Novalis and other classics of contemporary importance also take part in the drama. Perhaps the main theme of *Det* is the sacredness of life and continual creation, with allusions to modern physics and astrophysics, but also as a poetics of ethics. Parts of *Det* have been published in translation in French and American literary magazines, and complete translations into French and English exist but are not yet published. *Det* certainly belongs to world literature. I know of no other poetical work of the post-war years, not even in France, which speaks with such authority and such necessity. Since *Det* Inger Christensen has mostly worked as a playwright, rather too much influenced by Ionesco in her scenic and television works, but with great originality in a series of radio-plays, performed in several countries. In 1976 she published a long story *Det malede værelse* (The Painted Room), a marvellous recreation of the painter Mantegna and his decorations in the ducal palace of Mantua, in an intricately structured combination of Blixen's imaginative power and Borges' subtle wisdom. As a motto for the novel *Azorno* Inger Christensen used a sentence from Witold Gombrowicz' diaries: 'Man, as I see him, is 1) created by form, 2) creator of form, its untiring effectuator'. This is the double theme of the whole of her work, which can be seen as an original and important artistic animation of structuralism.

Equally subtle as a system-builder but perhaps not always equally successful is the novelist *Svend Aage Madsen* (1939, 1963) who is regarded in Denmark with almost the same reverence as Villy Sørensen. I have some serious reservations, but Madsen's ambitious and inventive series of big prose works is immensely impressive. His first books were perhaps rather too influenced by Beckett and the new French novel. In the late sixties he experimented with popular fiction for sophisticated purposes. In his increasingly longer books in the seventies he creates a fictional universe that is a strange combination of the Middle Ages, the Present and Science Fiction. The method is indicated in the title of the 1974-version, *Sæt verden er til*, which is both a request and an exclamation, both the philosophical 'Assume that the world exists!' and the naive exclamation 'What if the world exists!'. The tension of his latest novels is between experimental doubt and naive existence. I may perhaps be forgiven if it reminds me a little of a cross-breeding between Iris Murdoch and James Branch Cabell. Well, both are good story-tellers, and so is Madsen in his quirky way. But I have a more serious reservation. The two poles of the tension are the expression of an unbearable schizophrenic split and not of an artistic equilibrium. More librium than equi. Madsen's novels look like doodles to me, intricate and exceedingly intelligent labyrinths without an exit. They are obstinate attempts to adhere to the world, but they are ultimately without substance. I think my reaction shows that I have been scared by Madsen's books. And that might ultimately be what they want to achieve.

Schizophrenia as a literary method – an international fashion in the sixties – was also used with considerable success by *Ulla Ryum* (1937, 1962) and *Anders Westenholz* (1936, 1968), both absurdist novelists using psychoanalytic symbolism and experimental narrative technique in grotesque fables of sexual cruelty. Ryum started strongly with four short novels or novellas of which the second, *Natsangersken* (The

Night Singer) (1963) is the best. Her stories are beautiful, strange and grotesque, but perhaps too much of a literary drag show. She was influenced by Anaïs Nin and, especially, Djuna Barnes. It is the same obscure world which her characters inhabit. Westenholz is a psychologist by profession, and his three novels, *Polyp* (1968), *Martyrium* (1970) and *Det syvende æg* (The Seventh Egg) (1972) are almost clinical in their daring linguistic masochism. *Martyrium* is about a pregnant whore with persecution mania. So we know where we are. Ryum published two books of short stories in 1969 and 1971, but both she and Westenholz seem oppressed by the changes of fashion in literature. In the last few years both have started writing for the theatre, Ryum with great acclaim.

Changes of fashion have never oppressed *Sven Holm* (1940, 1961) who just changes with it. But then he is a very talented chameleon, whose many and unequal books show the development of prose fiction in the last fifteen years, not just his own. They are usually good to read, and sometimes very memorable. The only one which has been translated into English is *Termush, Atlanterhavskysten* (Termush, Atlantic Ocean) (1967), a serious science fiction story about the last men on earth. His absolutely best book is *Syg og munter* (Sick and Jolly) (1972), about a social loser in Copenhagen who is a psychiatric case, but with an interminable will to live. It is Holm's contribution to the new 'social' novel so much in demand, and it is better written than all the 'documentaries' and 'reports' by non-writers with too obvious messages as well as being infinitely more amusing. Holm is a versatile and intelligent, but still often curiously incoherent writer.

The very different sorts of imaginative, mostly non-realistic prose writers have been critically summed up, though I think wrongly, by the critic Thomas Bredsdorff under the label 'strange story-tellers', after Villy Sørensen's first book. The only thing common to Sørensen, Madsen, Holm, and the others is their lack of interest in non-style description of 'ordinary people'.

However, in the middle of the sixties a real group existed, though not for very long. The theoretical leader was the poet *Hans-Jørgen Nielsen* (1941, 1965) who promoted concrete poetry and a sort of pop-art aesthetics, which with journalistic flair he baptized 'attitudinal relativism'. MacLuhan and Warhol were its godparents and the German concrete poets its cousins. Nielsen himself wrote provocative and delightful essays and rather dry demonstrations in verse, but later turned to Marxist revivalism. The most talented poets of the group are *Per Kirkeby* (1938, 1966) and *Jørgen Leth* (1938, 1966). Both are better in other artistic fields, Kirkeby is our leading younger painter, and Leth is one of our best young filmmakers. But Kirkeby's collage technique and pictorial intelligence is used with good result in his books, too. And the cool, sensitive pop-art film language of Leth expresses itself engagingly in his books of poems and 'texts', some of them about sports, especially professional bicycling, which has also been the subject of some of his best feature films – and of his journalism, which is that rare phenomenon, sports journalism with literary qualities.

Vagn Steen (1928, 1964) is related to the concrete poets, but has another errand. He is a devil of a pedagogue, who uses poetry as one of many means – lectures, reviews, radio programs, children's books, pamphlets – to propagate his practical philosophy of culture and cultural politics. His most expressive expression of it in bookform was a little book containing nothing but blank pages, called *Skriv selv* (Write Yourself!) (1965). He is more interested in creative activity than in created works. In spite of this theory he often happens to write very fine poems. Another 'populist' is *Ebbe Reich* (1940, 1967) who belongs to the swampy middle-earth between literature and journalism. He is a fascinating personality who expresses himself with the same ease in poetry, novels, pseudo-biographies and articles on every imaginable current topic, spanning ideologically from Alistair Crowley to his contemporary Karl Marx. Reich's greatest success was *Frederik* (1972), a charming and superficial popular biography of Grundtvig, who was used among other things to support the crusade against Denmark's entry into the Common Market. Reich is an unscrupulous and very honest charlatan and a truly refreshing phenomenon on the cultural and political scene.

Among the new novelists at the end of the sixties only Knud Holten seems to me a truly important writer. Nevertheless *Kirsten Thorup* (1942, 1967) is very interesting. Her books indicate that the term 'attitudinal relativism' might after all be useful. Her two best books are both series of poetical texts, *Love from Trieste* (title in English) (1969) and *Idag er det Daisy* (Today It Is Daisy) (1971), fascinating montages of tenderness and cruelty in 'international' milieus, with a cutting technique which she has also used to advantage in some very good television plays. Thorup's theme is alienation and the reification of emotions, and her method, too, is alienation, in a cinematic language as burning as ice. *Baby* (1973), is an ambitious novel about sex and money, which aims to show that 'acts of violence are symptoms of a perverted society'. The same terrifying intensity of indirect social criticism as in Thorup, but not as cool and controlled, can be found in *Dorrit Willumsen's* (1940, 1965) books about unhappy, neurotic women who try to survive because there is nothing else to do.

Vagn Lundbye (1933, 1966) started as an orthodox French 'new novelist', later mixed in some American pop-art, but has lately taken on the rather curious role of a Danish Red Indian – promoting in fiction, essays and translations the cause of the American Indian, whose 'soul' Lundbye seems to communicate with. Another, perhaps sounder 'Indian' is *Ib Michael* (1945, 1970) who has studied Mexican Indian languages and written a very beautiful and unheroic travel-book, *Mayalandet* (Maya Country) (1973), combining facts with mythical knowledge. Michael's strictly fictional books are also mythical, the best being *Hjortefod* (Deerfoot) (1974), a post-Castaneda tale about the late Maximilian of Mexico. Another myth-maker is *Jens Smærup Sørensen* (1946, 1971), who after one book of poetry published a sensationally good first novel. His later prosebooks have been very assured, too, but not as strikingly original as *At ende som eneboer* (To End Up as a Hermit) (1972), a horrifying but very controlled story about the schizophrenia of a young man living both in a Danish suburb today (Smærup is a suburb specialist in his later books too) and in Mycenean Crete. Its dual psychologi-cal and mythical dramatization of the alienation/commit-ment syndrome in the literature of the seventies is marvel-lously well done.

Knud Holten (1945, 1966) is just a divine story-teller. He is as sensitive as the jazz-inspired Boris Vian and as serious as Le Clezio, in addition being as charming as younger Americans such as Brautigan and Tom Robbins, but neither cute nor coy. The four names mentioned indicate the type of writer he is, though he is not especially influenced by them – except perhaps by Vian – but thoroughly and delightfully original. Typically, he has written four books for children that are not very different from his adult books. His humour often has a wild nonsense about it that make Storm P. and Schade his Danish forbears. In his best books Holten plays with science fiction conventions, but he would not be accepted by ortho-dox science fiction fans, I'm afraid. Altogether, Holten is not for orthodox readers, but only for those select many who know that the flight of the imagination is not a way of escaping but a homecoming. *Englen med det langsomme smil* (The Angel with the Slow Smile) (1975) and *Feberfrihed* (Feverfree) (1977) are 'autobiographical' novels about a fic-tional character called Knud Holten in a fictional city called

Copenhagen, consisting of 'memories and miracles', the common title of the two novels. His best book to date is *Med hjertet i livet* (My Heart Leaps Up) (1972), a tremendous modern fairy tale in a science fiction milieu about distress, pollution and powerlessness contra youth, beauty and courage. It is Holten's most serious book, and it is very innocent and full of knowledge.

In many ways Holten's books can be seen as an expression of the new youth culture. So, too, can a whole group of very different poets who published their first books at the end of the sixties and might be termed 'the generation of '68' in memory of the revolt of that year, that may have failed but still means a great deal to many of us.

The least affected by that or any other revolution, except the one Baudelaire started, is *Henrik Nordbrandt* (1945, 1966), a 'pure' poet who with his first book, *Digte* (Poems) (1966) was hailed as a new classic. He is that rare phenomenon: a lyrical poet who cannot write a wrong line. The reader's risk is that the perfection of the poems overshadows their necessity. But this quality is present, too, in the 'decadent' sadness and desperation of the first books and in the increasingly sovereign acceptance of mutability and death in the later volumes, mainly 'about' Greece and Turkey, where Nordbrandt lives most of the time. The Byzantine themes and the grand, but intimate, style remind one of the last cycles of poems by Gunnar Ekelöf, Scandinavia's greatest modern poet (witness Auden and Sjöberg's congenial Penguin selection), though Nordbrandt is a very different temperament, more contemplative than eruptive. His sense of humour and humility also saves him from the pomposity that can attack other masters of the grand style, like Bjørnvig. In *Glas* (Glass – both the material and the container!) (1976) there are some perfectly intoxicating poems about intoxication, without the usual contrition of Dionysic verse, just pure sensuousness. Nordbrandt, the traveller, is an outsider but no refugee. A

Henrik Nordbrandt.

poem in *Opbrud og ankomster* (Departures and Arrivals) (1974), 'Foreign Cities' begins

> *Foreign cities look like life*
> *which I have never lived*
> *and which I therefore live*
> *when I experience them ...*

This typifies the wonder of his poetry, a sort of openness which is not a vacuum but empty-and-to-be-filled. Nordbrandt is a modern classic, at the age of thirty-two.

Klaus Høeck (1938, 1966) is another young poet who shows his attachment to the classics of modernist poetry – and also to the classics of rock music and science fiction. Primarily he works with computerized poetry, feeding datamats with linguistic material. These strange proceedings, common to composers, but rare among poets, have caused Høeck to be reproached for over-ambitiousness. Actually I do not see why a poet should not be ambitious in his work, and Høeck's poems are – where I can follow him without having to resort to his technical desriptions in appendices – poetry like any other poetry, only perhaps more so, quantitatively. His competence seems evident to my ignorance, but even better, his talent seems equally evident to my poetic knowledge. Høeck's first important book is a poem in five volumes called *Rejse* (Journey) (1971–73), an enormous trip, from Ancient Scandinavia to Space, from Homeric sky to cybernetic heat-death, with the truly ambitious project of 'writing the origin to its end'. Høeck's landscapes and skyscapes of words are formidable, and he can, through his method, suddenly focus on the tiniest beautiful detail. *Transformations* (1974) is, as the title indicates, computerized variations on texts, poems by the Swedo-Finnish Romantic Runeberg, Rilke, Valéry and Ezra Pound. From the latter Høeck quotes the good sentence 'Any fool can be spontaneous'. For his own part he demonstrates how the strictest self-assumed rules can create a *new* spontaneity. *Pentagram* (1976) uses the same methods to produce odes and hymns to rock groups such as Pink Floyd, Doors, Velvet Underground and the Rolling Stones – and is often as beautiful as their music. In *Projekt Perseus* (1977) his science fiction poetry really creates an unheard music. Klaus Høeck is not a 'specialty', but that much too rare phenomenon: a lyric poet who knows what he is doing.

Rolf Gjedsted (1947, 1969) might at first glance seem to be an example of the spontaneous 'any fool', but his easy style is very disciplined. If he was not exactly 'born with the blues' he at least grew up with rock and got high on all the psychedelic and esoteric phenomena associated with 'youth culture'. In some ways he expresses the disillusion of his generation when they found that the world was not that easy to change. But he is still a believer in magic, that is, the magic of poetry. He has sought out his modernistic predecessors – Baudelaire, Rimbaud, Trakl – and translated them and learnt from them in his own texts, the poems and prose poems approaching short stories in his many books, showing greater and greater technical command but also the maturing which one would like to find in his contemporaries, too. This Gjedsted does not seem to believe in, as a certain bitterness and isolationism in his later books indicate: the individual way is the only way, and it is painful and exacting. The 'beautiful people' disappeared, the 'beautiful world' was just a beautiful dream, and what is left is beautiful poetry and a certain emptiness. Gjedsted approaches these problems with great honesty and a non-moralistic mythical imagination that is very exciting. Like Knud Holten he accepts that he is a prisoner of his imagination, but that the imagination is free.

Among the other new poets of about '68 *Sten Kaalø* (1945, 1969) is the Danish Liverpool-poet, and as popular as his British colleagues once were, but with more humour and less sentimentality. *Lean Nielsen* (1935, 1969) is that rare phenomenon: the Original Working Class Poet, and as such is embraced by the wrong people for several wrong reasons, but he is a talented and powerful describer of survival against all odds. His diametrical opposite, the New (or even New New) Academic Poet, is *Per Aage Brandt* (1944, 1969) who while carrying the heavy burden of semiotics and Marxiotics has managed to write five collections of 'Poetry', as his books are called, not 'poems' but 'texts' in the French manner. His texts are illustrations of the connection between sex and economy in the capitalist world, seemingly practising Georges Bataille's theories. Brandt is a still better poet, I think, in his often incomprehensible but always overwhelmingly brilliant essays on literature. At least he is doing something which no-

117

body else does in Denmark, and which perhaps needs to be done. May it be done quickly!

Peter Laugesen (1942, 1968) is also familiar with modern French culture and anti-culture, but he uses it in a very original and definitely non-academic way. He is closest to Antonin Artaud, the mad theorist-poet. Laugesen, too, writes texts which are both poetry and theory, with an anarchistic frenzy that is unique in Danish literature, but has many parallels around the world today, in Lars Norén in Sweden, J. H. Prynne in England, Marcelin Pleynet and Denis Roche in France, for instance. Laugesen writes anti-poetry, a seemingly chaotic unfinished letter going on from book to book, with a feverish affirmation shining through all the brutal denials, an affirmation of language, of the Word. 'Poetry keeps chaos alive', he says in *Hamr & hak* (Strike & Chop) (1977), which is no different from his earlier regular books and his many underground pamphlets. Laugesen's books can be read both for their continual stream-of-anti-consciousness and for the detachable pieces of pure poetry, both for the thunder and the lightning.

Dan Turèll (1942, 1967), a friend and ally of Laugesen, is also an interminable writer, who after a discarded Pound-derivative first book has published more than fifty volumes in twelve years! Several of them are small pamphlets from underground presses with nice American names like 'Peace Eye Spirit' and 'Soft Machine Productions' (all of them his own enterprises). There are, however, many large books from commercial publishers, and even a bestseller and Book Club-success, *Vangede-billeder* (Vangede Pictures) (1975), a big collage of childhood memories of his suburban milieu, for which he was hailed as a New Realist, but which was rather a proof that he could do that, too, if he wanted to. Turèll seems to be able to do almost anything, he is frighteningly versatile, and does sometimes seem to think more of his image than of his imagery. Where Laugesen is a static writer repeating the

118

good message of Chaos, Turèll is dynamic. His heroes are Pound and Burroughs, Ginsberg and Turèll, and all the rock-and-roll stars from Chuck Berry to Lou Reed. So, of course, he professes an anti-intellectualism which his wide reading and deep understanding refute. He is into all the fads of the seventies, living off the fad of the land, so to say, but always at a cool aesthetic distance, it's there for the writing. He has a brutal charm, a tender charm and several other charms, and is an awfully bad influence on several of the younger poets. A book of more than 400 pages from 1972, with the appropriate title (I translate) 'Last Show Unconscious Trance Images of Exploding Mirror Tricks Through Flying Time Machine of Melting Electric Glass Photos' (we are in Burroughsland, the Disneyland of the hip) had an appendix with one of Turèll's most explicit statements of his poetics: 'As long as I don't want to obtain anything, as long as my writing is not imputed with any specific limitation through a "purpose", I (and it and you and yours) are invulnerable. He who is not cannot get hit. 'He who is not' is on the physical level, he who is not caught by random blocks of matter. What the power fears is the new invisible consciousness, the telepathy of silence in the streets.' There are some self-contradictions even in this short passage, and Turèll is a master of self-contradiction, but that is part of the game, and it is a good game. The strangest thing is that through the din of his millions of words he can actually make you hear – or feel – that telepathy of silence. He, too, wants to change his (your, my) life. He is a poet.

The Seventies

The seventies are over, but the history of the last ten years is too blurred to give any outline of them. All the young writers mentioned in the last chapter are functioning, as are several of the poets and novelists mentioned in earlier chapters and still alive and well and publishing. But it must be admitted that there has been a scarcity of talented new writers in the seventies, partly owing perhaps to the economic decline after the affluence of the sixties. However Danish publishers are more generous towards first books than publishers in most other countries. The general cultural climate has been rather hard, too, with the official debate in newspapers and magazines mostly being between different fractions of Marxism, either simply discarding literature as 'bourgeois' or demanding and artificially promoting a 'working class literature', which has not until now produced any striking talents. Likewise, the women's liberation movement has acquired the right for female writers to publish anything, irrespective of literary quality. And the popular and critical successes have very often been books without any literary merits, but bringing fuel to political discussions.

In spite of all this, new talents have emerged, and the greatest of them is *Marianne Larsen* (1951, 1971). Like Dan Turèll – who in his latest books of poetry with journalistic verve has paid tribute to the ruling populism – she practises the 'telepathy of silence'. Silence as a theme is almost an obsession with Marianne Larsen, but she has slowly up through the seventies developed her theme from a neurotic solipsism to a necessary community of silence. She has moved from the silence of anguish to the silence of love. *Fællessprog* (Common-Language) is the title of one of her best books (1975). She is one of the few new writers for whom political commitment is not an excuse for inadequacy. She is still very young, but she speaks with the authority of the true poet – which by a majority of the left-wing cultural elite is naively taken as 'authoritarian' – and she has important things to say.

Another version of 'poésie engagée' is the one practised by *Eske K. Mathiesen* (1944, 1976) in three very good collections of poetry. Mathiesen is not only a communist, he is also an art critic and, most important, a folklorist by profession. He translates non-European folk poetry, and he 'imitates' Danish folk poetry and seems to be the latest follower of a – never defined – popular trend through Danish poetry from the medieval ballads and the juicier texts of the Low Baroque, through both Grundtvig and Aarestrup and onwards through Aakjær and up to Frank Jæger. His consciousness of tradition is very non-traditional and very exciting, and it indicates a will to communicate, the result of which is not folksiness but a new and very lovely simplicity.

Among the new prose writers *Inge Eriksen* (1935, 1975) has published a six-hundred-page long novel, *Victoria og verdensrevolutionen* (Victoria and the World Revolution) (1976) which is a very clever imitation of the old-fashioned popular novel, with a beautiful heroine and a lot of strong, good heroes, who work, play, fight and make love in an imaginary Latin American country between or simultaneously with endless political discussions. It is a terribly irritating and enormously vital book. Another first novel, *Kassander* (1975) by *Claus Bech* (1943) uses the conventions of the popular novel with more sophistication, a little like the late Robbe-Grillet. Under the spy story surface Kassander is a philosophical demonstration that we are the fate of our neighbours.

Several other new writers could be given honourable mention and I do not want to close on a pessimistic note. My disparaging remarks about the populist tendencies of the last ten years are of course coloured by my own aesthetics, and it is not foolproof.

But the tide is turning again! Among the latest newcomers in Danish literature I seem to find a return to the metaphorical – and perhaps metaphysical – commitment of the forties, but of course with new aspects. It is rather strange to quote David Bowie as the greatest influence on young Danish poets, but it is a fact. *F. P. Jac* (a pseudonym, 1955, 1976) made his official début in 1978 with *Munden brænder på huden* (The

Mouth Burns On the Skin), but already in 1976, in a small underground pamphlet, he heralded the coming of the eighties and raved against 'the authoritarian flags and pennants / that stamped the seventies as scared adolescent times'. And he announced a new life-giving poetry:

lad bierne suge honningen fra din kærligheds kropsblad
lad menneskene knuse deres ærgerrige negle
når vor nytænkning blomstrer ud af sommereftermiddagen
der skal pudse 80erne af som motiverede

(let the bees suck the honey from the body-petal of your love / let people crush their ambitious nails / when our new-thinking blossoms out of the summer afternoon / which shall polish the eighties as motivated).

We look forward to that! As F. P. Jac says in another poem in his first pamphlet, 'På gensyn i fremsyn', 'See you again in pre-vision' – or 'far-sight' (far out!) – or simply 'vision'. Literature is, like criticism, what John Cowper Powys called his first book of essays: Visions and Revisions.

Bibliography

of Danish literature and literary history

A select list compiled with the assistance of the Danish Department of the Royal Library, Copenhagen

The bibliography is mainly based on material in the Royal Library, the national library of Denmark, and most of the recent literature has been selected from Dania Polyglotta, a bibliography published annually by the Royal Library and comprising literature on Denmark in English (and other world languages) and translations of Danish literature. For the complete title of this bibliography see below under the heading 'Bibliography'. While the present bibliography is highly selective, the Dania Polyglotta aims at being complete and should therefore be consulted by all who wish to undertake more extensive research.

When a book has gone into several editions the most recent edition has been preferred as being more easily available to the public; for historical reasons, however, the year of the first edition in English has been added in square brackets.

Anthologies

Anthology of Danish literature. Ed. by F. J. Billeskov Jansen and P. M. Mitchell. Carbondale, Ill. Southern Illinois Univ. Pr. 1971. 606 p.

Contemporary Danish plays. Freeport, N.Y. Books for Libraries Pr. 1970. 556 p. [Reprint of 1955 ed.].

Contemporary Danish poetry. Boston, Mass. Twayne. 1977. 343 p.

Contemporary Danish prose. Westport, Conn. Greenwood Pr. 1974. 375 p. [Reprint of 1958 ed.].

Danish ballads. Cambridge. 1920. 166 p.

Danish ballads and folk songs. Selected and ed. by Erik Dal. Ill. by Marcel Rasmussen. Cph. Rosenkilde og Bagger. 1967. 303 p. ill.

Denmark's best stories. Ed. by Hanne Astrup Larsen. New York. 1928. 377 p.

The devil's instrument and other Danish stories. Ed. by Sven Holm. London. Owen. 1971. 266 p.

Faroese short stories. Introduction and notes by Hedin Brønner. New York. Twayne. 1972. 267 p.

Five modern Scandinavian plays. New York. Twayne. 1971. 424 p.

Four-and-forty. A selection of Danish ballads presented in Scots. Edinburgh. 1954. 184 p.

Historical ballads of Denmark. Ill. by Edward Bawden and George Mackie. Edinburgh. 1958. 158 p. ill.

Modern Danish authors. Ed. by Evelyn Heepe and Niels Heltberg. Folcroft, Pa. Folcroft Library Editions. 1974. 222 p. [Reprint of 1946 ed.].

Modern Nordic plays: Denmark. Oslo. Universitetsforlaget. 1974. 449 p.

The royal guest – and other classical Danish narrative. Ed. by P. M. Mitchell and Kenneth H. Ober. Chicago, Ill. Univ. of Chicago Pr. 1977. 242 p.

Bibliography

Bredsdorff, Elias: Danish literature in English translation. With a special Hans Christian Andersen supplement. A bibliography. Westport, Conn. Greenwood Pr. 1973. 198 p. [Reprint of 1950 ed.].

Dania polyglotta. Literature on Denmark in languages other than Danish & Books of Danish interest published abroad. An annual bibliography compiled by the Danish Department of the Royal Library. New series. 1969–. Cph. The Royal Library. 1970–. [Annual].

Denmark. A bibliography. With a special section on Hans Christian Andersen. Ed. by Sven C. Jacobsen, Karsten Kromann, Jan William Rasmussen. 2. ed. Cph. The Royal Library. 1976. 56 p. [1975].

Literary history

Abrahamsen, Povl & Erik Dal: The Heart Book. The tradition of the Danish ballad. Cph. Ministry of Foreign Affairs. 1965. 41 p. ill.

Bredsdorff, Elias, Brita Mortensen & Ronald G. Popperwell: An introduction to Scandinavian literature. Westport, Conn. Greenwood Pr. 1970. 245 p. [Reprint of 1951 ed.].

Brønner, Hedin: Three Faroese novelists. An appreciation of Jørgen-Frantz Jacobsen, William Heinesen and Heðin Brú. New York. Twayne. 1973. 140 p.

Fenger, Henning & Frederick J. Marker: The Heibergs. New York. Twayne. 1971. 191 p.

Jones, W. Glyn: Faroe and cosmos. Newcastle. Univ. of Newcastle upon Tyne. 1974. 18 p.

Leach, Henry Goddard: Angevin Britain and Scandinavia. New York. Kraus. 1975. 432 p. [Reprint of 1921 ed.].

Mitchell, P. M.: A history of Danish literature. 2. ed. New York. Kraus-Thomsen. 1971. 339 p. ill. [1957].

Scandinavian studies. The journal of the Society for the Advancement of Scandinavian Study. Lawrence, Kan. 1911–. [Periodical].

Scandinavica. An international journal of Scandinavian studies. London. Academic Pr. 1962–. [Periodical].

Scandinavica. Special issue devoted to contemporary Scandinavian poetry. London. Academic Pr. 1973. 139 p.

Steenstrup, Johannes C. H. R.: The medieval popular ballad. Seattle, Wash. Univ. of Washington Pr. 1968. 28 + 269 p. [1914].

The types of the Scandinavian medieval ballad. Oslo. Universitetsforlaget. 1978. 329 p.

Individual authors

Aakjær, Jeppe (1866–1930)
Songs of the heath. Llanfairfechan. H. Glyn Davies. 1962. 42 p.

Abell, Kjeld (1901–61)
The melody that got lost. London. 1939. 99 p.
Three from Minikoi. London. Secker and Warburg. 1960. 319 p.
– – –
Marker, Frederick J.: Kjeld Abell. Boston, Mass. Twayne. 1976. 172 p.

Andersen, Benny (b. 1929)
Selected poems. Princeton, N. J. Princeton Univ. Pr. 1975. 141 p.

Andersen, Hans Christian (1805–75)
Ardizzone's Hans Andersen. Ill. by Edward Ardizzone. London. Deutsch. 1978. 191 p. ill.
The complete fairy tales and stories. New York. Doubleday. 1974. 1101 p.

Fairy tales and legends. Ill. by Rex Whistler. London. Bodley Head. 1978. 470 p. ill. [1935].

Rome, or the improvisatore. New York. 1894. 414 p. ill. [1845].

– – –

Bredsdorff, Elias: A bibliography of Hans Christian Andersen's works in English translation and of books and articles relating to H. C. Andersen. (Elias Bredsdorff: Danish literature in English translation. Westport, Conn. Greenwood Pr. 1973. p. 119–198 [Reprint of 1950 ed.]).

Hans Christian Andersen. (Denmark. A bibliography. Ed. by Sven C. Jacobsen, Karsten Kromann, Jan William Rasmussen. 2. ed. Cph. The Royal Library. 1976. p. 52–56. [1975]).

– – –

Andersen, Hans Christian: The fairy tale of my life. An autobiography. New York. Paddington Pr. 1975. 569 p. ill. [1871]

Andersen, Hans Christian: Pictures of travel in Sweden, among the Hartz mountains, and in Switzerland, with a visit at Charles Dickens's house. New York. 1871. 293 p.

Andersen, Hans Christian: A poet's bazaar. Pictures of travel in Germany, Italy, Greece and the Orient. New York. 1871. 343 p. [1846].

Bredsdorff, Elias: Hans Andersen and Charles Dickens. A friendship and its dissolution. Cph. Rosenkilde og Bagger. 1956. 140 p. ill.

Bredsdorff, Elias: Hans Christian Andersen. London. Phaidon Pr. 1975. 344 p. ill.

Faaborg, N. L.: Hans Christian Andersen portraits in graphic representation. Cph. The Royal Library. 1971. 56 p. ill.

Heltoft, Kjeld: Hans Christian Andersen as an artist. Cph. Ministry of Foreign Affairs. 1977. 143 p. ill.

Spink, Reginald: Hans Christian Andersen and his world. London. Thames and Hudson. 1972. 128 p. ill.

Andersen Nexø, Martin (1869–1954)

Ditte. Gloucester, Mass. Peter Smith. 1963. 1 vol. [1920–1923].

In God's land. New York. 1933. 343 p.

Pelle the Conqueror. Vol. 1–4. London. 1913–1916. 4 vols.

– – –

Andersen Nexø, Martin: Days in the sun. London. 1929. 297 p.

Andersen Nexø, Martin: Under the open sky. My early years. New York. 1938. 330 p.

Bang, Herman (1857–1912)
Denied a country. New York. 1927. 365 p.
Ida Brandt. New York. 1926. 311 p.

Blicher, Steen Steensen (1782–1848)
Diary of a parish clerk. Ill. by Jørgen C. Rasmussen. Herning. Poul
Kristensen. 1976. 114 p. ill.
Twelve stories. New York. Kraus. 1972. 305 p. [Reprint of 1945 ed.].

Blixen, Karen (1885–1962)
Anecdotes of destiny. By Isak Dinesen [pseud.]. London. Univ. of
Chicago Pr. 1976. 244 p. [1958].
The angelic avengers. By Isak Dinesen [pseud.]. Chicago, Ill. Univ.
of Chicago Pr. 1976. 304 p. [1946].
Carnival. Entertainments and posthumous tales. By Isak Dinesen
[pseud.]. London. Heinemann. 1977. 338 p.
Ehrengard. By Isak Dinesen [pseud.]. New York. Vintage Books.
1975. 111 p. [1963].
Last tales. By Isak Dinesen [pseud.]. London. Univ. of Chicago Pr.
1976. 341 p. [1957].
Seven gothic tales. By Isak Dinesen [pseud.]. St. Albans. Triad. 1979.
352 p. [1934].
Winter's tales. By Isak Dinesen [pseud.]. London. Univ. of Chicago
Pr. 1976. 313 p. [1942].
– – –

Henriksen, Liselotte: Isak Dinesen. A bibliography. Cph. Gyldendal. 1977. 224 p.
– – –

Blixen, Karen: Out of Africa. Harmondsworth. Penguin. 1979.
329 p. [1937].
Blixen, Karen: Shadows on the grass. By Isak Dinesen [pseud.]. London. Univ. of Chicago Pr. 1976. 149 p. [1960].
Dinesen, Thomas: My sister, Isak Dinesen. London. Joseph. 1975.
127 p. ill.
Hannah, Donald: 'Isak Dinesen' and Karen Blixen. The mask and
the reality. London. Putnam. 1971. 218 p. ill.
Langbaum, Robert: Isak Dinesen's art. Chicago, Ill. Univ. of Chicago Pr. 1975. 309 p.

Lasson, Frans & Clara Svendsen: The life and destiny of Karen Blixen. London. Joseph. 1970. 227 p. ill.

Trzebinski, Errol: Silence will speak. A study of the life of Denys Finch Hatton and his relationship with Karen Blixen. London. Heinemann. 1977. 348 p. ill.

Bodelsen, Anders (b. 1937)
Consider the verdict. New York. Harper & Row. 1976. 276 p.
Freezing point. London. Joseph. 1971. 174 p.
Hit and run, run, run. Harmondsworth. Penguin. 1971. 219 p. [1970].
The silent partner. Harmondsworth. Penguin. 1978. 221 p. [1969].
Straus. New York. Harper & Row. 1974. 147 p.

Bødker, Cecil (b. 1927)
The leopard. New York. Atheneum. 1975. 186 p.

Brandes, Georg (1842–1927)
Main currents in 19th century literature. Vol. 1–6. London. 1901–1905. 6 vols.

– – –

Brandes, Georg: Reminiscences of my childhood and youth. New York. Arno Pr. 1975. 397 p. [Reprint of 1906 ed.].
Nolin, Bertil: Georg Brandes. Boston, Mass. Twayne. 1976. 208 p.

Brandt, Jørgen Gustava (b. 1929)
Tête à tête. Willimantic, Conn. Curbstone Pr. 1978. 31 p.

Branner, H. C. (1903–66)
No man knows the night. London. 1958. 301 p.
The riding master. London. 1951. 159 p.
The story of Börge. New York. Twayne. 1973. 196 p.
Two minutes of silence. Madison, Wisc. Univ. of Wisconsin Pr. 1966. 211 p.

– – –

Markey, T. L.: H. C. Branner. New York. Twayne. 1973. 186 p.

Brú, Heðin
see Jacobsen, Hans Jacob

Dinesen, Isak
see Blixen, Karen

Dreyer, Carl Th. (1889–1968)
Four screenplays. London. Thames and Hudson. 1970. 312 p. ill.

128

Ewald, Carl (1856–1908)
The battle of the bees and other stories. Ill. by Lily R. Phillips, New York. Crane Russak. 1977. 114 p. ill.
My little boy. My big girl. New York. Horizon Pr. 1962. 190 p.

Ewald, Johannes (1743–81)
The death of Balder. London. 1889. 77 p.

Gjellerup, Karl (1857–1919)
Minna. London. 1913. 340 p.
The pilgrim Kamanita. London. 1911. 305 p.

Goldschmidt, M. A. (1819–87)
Homeless. Vol. 1–3. London. 1861. 3 vols.
Jacob Bendixen, the Jew. Vol. 1–3. London. 1852. 3 vols.
– – –

Ober, Kenneth H.: Meîr Goldschmidt. Boston, Mass. Twayne. 1976. 146 p. ill.

Gress, Elsa (b. 1919)
Philoctetes wounded and other plays. Glumsø. 1969. 168 p. ill.

Grundtvig, N. F. S. (1783–1872)
Selected writings. Ed. by Johannes Knudsen. Philadelphia, Pa. Fortress Pr. 1976. 184 p.
– – –

Thaning, Kaj: N. F. S. Grundtvig. Cph. Det danske Selskab. 1972. 175 p. ill.
Knudsen, Johannes: Danish rebel. A study of N. F. S. Grundtvig. Philadelphia, Pa. 1955. 242 p.
Koch, Hal: Grundtvig. Yellow Springs, Ohio. 1952. 231 p.
Lindhardt, P. G.: Grundtvig. London. 1951. 141 p.

Hansen, Martin A. (1909–55)
Against the wind. New York. Ungar. 1979.
The liar. New York. Twayne. 1969. 205 p.
Lucky Kristoffer. New York. Twayne. 1974. 377 p.
– – –

Ingwersen, Faith & Niels: Martin A. Hansen. Boston, Mass. Twayne. 1976. 197 p. ill.

Hansen, Thorkild (b. 1927)
Arabia Felix. The Danish expedition of 1761–1767. London. Collins. 1964. 381 p. ill.
North West to Hudson Bay. The life and times of Jens Munk. London. Collins. 1970. 378 p. ill.

Hauch, Carsten (1790–1872)
Robert Fulton. New York. 1868. 450 p.

Heiberg, P. A. (1758–1841)
Poverty and wealth. London. 1799. 83 p.

Hein, Piet (b. 1905)
Grooks, Vol. 1–5. Garden City, N.Y. Doubleday. 1969–1973. 5 vols. ill.

Heinesen, William (b. 1900)
The kingdom of the earth. New York. Twayne. 1974. 171 p.
The lost musicians. New York. Twayne. 1971. 364 p.
Niels Peter. London. 1939. 316 p.

– – –

Jones, W. Glyn: William Heinesen. New York. Twayne. 1974. 201 p.

Hertz, Henrik (1797–1870)
King René's daughter. 3. ed., rev. New York. 1904. 100 p. [1845].

Holberg, Ludvig (1684–1754)
Comedies. New York. 1935. 178 p.
Four plays. Princeton, N. J. 1946. 202 p.
An introduction to universal history. London. 1787. 354 p. [1755].
A journey to the world underground. New York. Garland. 1974. 324 p. [1742].
Peder Paars. Lincoln, Neb. Univ. of Nebraska Pr. 1962. 193 p. ill.
Selected essays. Lawrence, Kan. 1955. 166 p.
Seven one-act plays. Millwood, N.Y. Kraus. 1972. 205 p. [Reprint of 1950 ed.].
Three comedies. London. 1912. 207 p.
Three comedies. London. 1957. 91 p.

– – –

Billeskov Jansen, F. J.: Ludvig Holberg. New York. Twayne. 1974. 135 p.

Campbell, Oscar James: The comedies of Holberg. New York. Blom. 1968. 363 p. [1914].

Ludvig Holberg's Memoirs. An eighteenth century Danish contribution to international understanding. Ed. by Stewart E. Fraser. Leiden. Brill. 1970. 289 p. ill.

Holm, Sven (b. 1940)
Termush. London. Faber & Faber. 1969. 110 p.

Ingemann, B. S. (1789–1862)
The childhood of King Erik Menved. London. 1846. 390 p.
The outlaws and King Eric. Vol. 1–3. London. 1850. 3 vols.
Waldemar surnamed Seir, or the Victorious. Vol. 1–3. London. 1841. 3 vols.

Jacobsen, Hans Jacob (b. 1901)
The old man and his sons. By Heðin Brú [pseud.]. New York. Eriksson. 1970. 203 p.

Jacobsen, J. P. (1847–85)
Marie Grubbe. 2. ed. Boston, Mass. Twayne. 1975. 261 p. [1917].
Mogens and other stories. New York. 1921. 150 p.
Niels Lyhne. New York. Twayne. 1967. 244 p. [1896].
Poems. Oxford. 1920. 27 p.

Jacobsen, Jørgen-Frantz (1900–38)
Barbara. Harmondsworth. 1948. 246 p.

Jensen, Johannes V. (1873–1950)
The fall of the king. London. 1933. 286 p.
The long journey. New York. Knopf. 1961. 677 p. [1922–1924].
The waving rye. Cph. 1958. 153 p.

Jørgensen, Johannes (1866–1956)
Jones, W. Glyn: Johannes Jörgensen. New York. Twayne. 1969. 183 p.

Kierkegaard, Søren (1813–55)
Either/or. Vol. 1–2. Princeton, N. J. Princeton Univ. Pr. 1971. 2 vols. [1944].
Stages on life's way. Princeton, N. J. 1945. 472 p. [1940].
– – –

Lowrie, Walter: Kierkegaard. Vol. 1–2. Gloucester, Mass. Smith. 1970. 640 p. ill.
Mackey, Louis: Kierkegaard: A kind of poet. Philadelphia, Pa. Univ. of Philadelphia Pr. 1971. 327 p.
Stendahl, Brita K.: Søren Kierkegaard. Boston, Mass. Twayne. 1976. 235 p.
Brandt, Frithiof: Søren Kierkegaard. 1813–1855. His life – his works. Cph. Det danske Selskab. 1963. 110 p.

Kristensen, Tom: (1893–1974)
Havoc. Madison, Wisc. Univ. of Wisconsin Pr. 1968. 425 p.

Malinovski, Ivan (b. 1926)
Critique of silence. Cph. Gyldendal. 1977. 78 p.

Munk, Kaj (1898–1944)
Five plays. 2. pr. Kbh. Nyt Nordisk Forlag. 1964. 272 p. [1953].

Nielsen, Jørgen (1902–45)
The will of the heart. Cph. Wind-flower Pr. 1979. 21 p.

Nordbrandt, Henrik (b. 1945)
Selected poems. Willimantic, Conn. Curbstone Pr. 1978. 83 p.

Oehlenschläger, Adam (1779–1850)
Aladdin or The wonderful lamp. Cph. Gyldendal. 1968. 297 p. [1857].
Axel and Valborg. London. 1874. 164 p. [1841].
Correggio. Edinburgh. 1865. 87 p. [1846].
Earl Hakon the Mighty. London. 1874. 172 p. [1840].
The gods of the North. London. 1845. 372 p.
The gold horns. London. 1913. 25 p.
Palnatoke. London. 1855. 65 p.

Ørum, Poul (b. 1919)
Nothing but the truth. London. Gollancz. 1976. 253 p.
Scapegoat. New York. Pantheon. 1975. 255 p.
The whipping-boy. London. Gollancz. 1975. 255 p.

Paludan, Jacob (1896–1976)
Birds around the light. New York. 1928. 347 p.
Jørgen Stein. Madison, Wisc. Univ. of Wisconsin Pr. 1966. 724 p.

Panduro, Leif (1923–77)
Kick me in the traditions. New York. Eriksson-Taplinger. 1961. 217 p.
One of our millionaires is missing. New York. Grove Pr. 1967. 174 p.

Petersen, Nis (1897–1943)
Spilt milk. London. 1935. 297 p.
The street of the sandalmakers. London. 1933. 496 p.

Pontoppidan, Henrik (1857–1943)
The apothecary's daughter. London. 1890. 153 p.
Emanuel or Children of the soil. Ill. by Nelly Erichsen. London. 1896. 307 p. ill.
The promised land. Ill. by Nelly Erichsen. London. 1896. 285 p. ill.
– – –
Mitchell, P. M.: Henrik Pontoppidan. Boston, Mass. Twayne. 1979. 158 p.

Rasmussen, Halfdan (b. 1915)
Halfdanes nonsense and nursery rhymes. Ill. by Ernst Clausen, Ib Spang Olsen and Arne Ungermann. Kbh. Schønberg. 1973. 52 p. ill.

Rifbjerg, Klaus (b. 1931)
Selected poems. Willimantic, Conn. Curbstone Pr. 1976. 36 p.

Ryum, Ulla (b. 1937)
The saddened ventriloquist. Cph. Radio Denmark. 1971. 46 p.

Sarvig, Ole (b. 1921)
Late day. Ill. by Palle Nielsen. Willimantic, Conn. Curbstone Pr. 1976. 43 p. ill.

Saxo Grammaticus (c. 1150–c. 1220)
The first nine books of the history of Saxo Grammaticus. Vol. 1–2. London. 1905. 2 vols. ill. [1894].

Schade, Jens August (1903–78)
People meet and sweet music fills the heart. New York. Dell. 1969. 188 p.

Scherfig, Hans (1905–79)
The 'idealists'. London. 1949. 224 p.

Skou-Hansen, Tage (b. 1925)
The naked trees. London. 1959. 222 p.

Sørensen, Villy (b. 1929)
Tiger in the kitchen and other strange stories. Freeport, N.Y. Books for Libraries Pr. 1969. 204 p. [1956].

Soya, C. E. (b. 1896)
Farmor's house. Cph. Borgen. 1964. 293 p.
Seventeen. Part 1–3. London. Sphere Books. 1969. 2 vols.

Ulfeldt, Leonora Christina (1621–98)
Ulfeldt, Leonora Christina: Memoirs of Leonora Christina, daughter of Christian IV of Denmark. London. 1929. 342 p. [1872].

Wied, Gustav (1858–1914)
$2 \times 2 = 5$. New York. 1923. 146 p.

List of Illustrations

Index of Danish Authors

137

139

What can we learn from one another?

Aim and work of the Danish Institute

Det danske Selskab, The Danish Institute is an independent nonprofit institution for cultural exchange between Denmark and other countries. Abroad its aims is to inform other countries about life and culture in Denmark, particularly in the field of education, welfare services and other branches of sociology; at home to help spread knowledge of cultural affairs in other countries. Its work of information is thus based on the idea of mutuality and treated as a comparative study of cultural development at home and abroad by raising the question: What can we learn from one another? The work of the Danish Institute is done mainly in three ways:

1) By branches of the Danish Institute abroad – in Great Britain (Edinburgh), the Benelux countries (Brussels), France (Rouen), Switzerland (Zürich), Italy (Milan), West Germany (Dortmund) and its contacts in the USA and other countries. Lectures, reference work, the teaching of Danish, exhibitions, concerts, film shows, radio and television programmes as well as study tours and summer schools are an important part of the work of representatives of the Institutes that have been established abroad.

2) Summer seminars and study tours both in Denmark and abroad. Participants come from Denmark and other countries. The study tours bring foreign experts to Denmark and take Danish experts abroad. Teachers, librarians, architects and persons engaged in social welfare and local government make up a large part.

3) Publication of books and reference papers in foreign languages. Primary and Folk High Schools in Denmark, the library system, welfare services, cooperative movement, handicrafts, architecture, literature, art and music, life and work of prominent Danes are among the main subjects.

The author Martin A. Hansen called the Danish Institute a Folk High School beyond the borders: »In fact the work of the Danish Institute abroad has its roots in our finest traditions of popular education, which go right back to Grundtvig and Kold. The means and methods used are modern, the materials the very best and the approach to the work is cultural in the truest meaning of the word.«

DET DANSKE SELSKAB

*The Danish Institute for Information about Denmark and
Cultural Cooperation with other Nations*

KULTORVET 2, DK-1175 COPENHAGEN, DENMARK

Publications in English:

DANISH INFORMATION HANDBOOKS

Schools and Education – The Danish Folk High Schools –
Special Education in Denmark – Public Libraries in Denmark
– Social Welfare in Denmark – Local Government in Denmark
– The Danish Cooperative Movement

DENMARK IN PRINT AND PICTURES

The Danish Church – Danish Architecture – Danish Painting
and Sculpture – Danish Design – Industrial Life in Denmark –
The Story of Danish Film – Sport in Denmark – Garden Colonies in Denmark – Copenhagen, Capital of a Democracy –
Aarhus, Meeting Place of Tradition and Progress – The Lim-
fjord, its Towns and People

In preparation:

Funen, the Heart of Denmark

DANES OF THE PRESENT AND PAST

Danish Literature – Contemporary Danish Composers – Arne
Jacobsen, by P. E. Skriver – Søren Kierkegaard, by Frithiof
Brandt – N. F. S. Grundtvig, by Kaj Thaning

DANISH REFERENCE PAPERS

The Danish Mother's Aid Centres – Employers and Workers –
The Ombudsman – Care of the Aged in Denmark

PERIODICALS

Contact with Denmark. Published annually in English, French,
German, Italian, Netherlandish.
Musical Denmark, nos. 1–30. Published annually in English.